Published by
Renu Kaul Verma
Vitasta Publishing Pvt Ltd
2/15, Ansari Road, Daryaganj
New Delhi-110 002
info@vitastapublishing.com

ISBN 978-93-90961-91-7

First Edition 2022

MRP ₹ 695

Edited by Dhanalakshmi Ayyer, Mansi Bisht
Cover and Layout by Somesh Kumar Mishra
Printed by Chaman Enterprises, New Delhi

PANDEMIC DISRUPTIONS AND ODISHA'S LESSONS IN GOVERNANCE

PUBLIC HEALTH, DATA PROTECTION AND OTHER ESSAYS

DR AMAR PATNAIK

Vitasta

PANDEMIC DISRUPTIONS AND ODISHA'S LESSONS IN GOVERNANCE

CONTENTS

PREFACE

This book is a culmination of the various essays that I wrote on pertinent contemporary issues that emerged in India during the pandemic years of 2020-21 and 2021-2022. Since the pandemic struck the world, many fissures emerged which needed to be analysed to understand where India stood in the world. They pertained to healthcare, vaccines, online education for children as schools and colleges shut down and the increasing use of technology to mitigate these concerns. With the use of technology, there was emergence of the issue of data privacy and citizen's right to privacy.

Added to these was also the issue of disaster management and the state's capacity to negotiate these on a sustainable basis even as financial and budgetary resources of both the Centre and State were dwindling. This book is a commentary on these topics with some concrete suggestions as to how either policy planning or implementation of policy could have been better during that extant period. The essays also cover India's fight with the pandemic, the economic concerns of the country, the use and future of artificial intelligence, blockchain technology, environmental concerns, and Odisha's success trajectory in this turmoil, etc.

Health

The essays focus on COVID management and India's health infrastructure. The COVID-19 crisis provided a glimpse of what a full-scale public health response can look like and the yawning gap in India's current health infrastructure to meet the same. Odisha which is experienced at tackling cyclones, adopted a disaster management approach and mobilised resources more effectively than most states.

The State decentralised its approach by empowering and trusting Panchayat systems to manage temporary quarantine centres which, prevented pressure on the formal health system. However, there is a need to promote equity in the health system so that healthcare costs do not become a financial burden on the poor which currently accounts for more than 40% of his earning. The essays cover discussion on the vaccine policy in detail as it evolved with the various waves of the pandemic. Need for IPR relaxations for vaccine manufacture in which India, South Africa and New Zealand took lead has also been discussed.

Technology

Under this category, I analyse how there is a need to protect consumers from the misuse of artificial intelligence as these systems rely on big data sets which contain a mixture of personal and non-personal data. In case the data set is biased, it will lead to biased AI decision-making leading to discrimination and prejudice towards a certain class of consumers, price discrimination and undue influence over their choices and reactions. Hence, there is a need to regulate the adoption and use of AI. These regulations must be optimal, dynamic, evidence based and light touch regulations with elements of self-regulation. At the same time, adoption of AI for improving economy, efficiency and effectiveness of Government/public services should be aggressively encouraged and pursued.

Child Rights

The impact of COVID on women and children had long lasting effects. The NHRC 'Advisory for Protection of the Rights of Children in the context of Covid-19' did not address the socio-economic needs of children becoming orphans due to COVID as well as non-recognition of universal access to nutritional services for children outside the ICDS framework. The pandemic made more girls vulnerable to child marriages and trafficking. This not only is a violation of their human rights but also pushes them into a vicious cycle of poverty. I have covered this aspect elaborately in my essays.

Odisha's achievements

The book also sheds light on Odisha and its transformation from being a disaster-prone State to being a leader in disaster management. I underline how the lessons Odisha learnt from preventing deaths during cyclones were successfully used to prevent loss of life during the COVID pandemic. Odisha relies on a 5T approach to governance: technology and leveraging it, transparency in governance, team work from the various stakeholders involved and meeting targets in a time-bound manner, thereby leading to transformation.

Data Protection

Right to Privacy and Data Protection lays down my analysis of how data should be regulated in the country, particularly relevant as Central Government introduced a bill named Personal Data Protection Bill in December 2019 in the Parliament. It was done in light of the landmark Puttuswamy judgement (2017) which enshrined the right to privacy as a fundamental right under Article 21. The essays argue that non-personal data should be governed only through light-touch regulations to allow for development of the market whereas privacy of citizen's personal data should be ensured through a tight consent-based and accountability centred legislative architecture based on the principles laid down by the Hon'ble Supreme Court in the aforesaid judgement. However, since it is impossible to have a watertight distinction between the personal and non-personal data, a case is made out for a single Data Protection Authority for both personal and non-personal data. There is also a need for separate national and state level data protection authorities to make the administration of data protection regime more robust, implementable and beyond disputes over powers of the Central and the States to investigate complaints and impose penalties.

Economy

India's economy took a hit during the COVID pandemic years when the country initially went into a complete lockdown. Since then, two budgets have been passed which seek to revive the economy. This book brings forth essays which scrutinise India's response to economically empower the citizenry and the States through budgetary allocations. Budget FY 2021 which focused a great deal on capex, fell short of ensuring equity, both federal and citizen. The over-reliance of the central government on cess and surcharge have also increased the borrowing requirement of States leading to increasing federal inequity. Here, I evaluate whether only a strong push for capex is the right direction for a country to recover the losses it has suffered due to the pandemic or more is required to be done in social sectors to bridge the inequities in wealth and income while making an economic recovery.

Environment

India has been blessed with not just biodiversity hotspots but also a varied biome. It becomes our responsibility to ensure that this heritage is protected for the future generations. In this context, I examined the draft Environment Impact Assessment (EIA) notification 2020 which shifts from "polluter pays principle" to "pollute and pay" principle. The battle with the current pandemic has made it very clear how vulnerable and unstable our systems of production, distribution and supply are in the face of nature. Therefore, it is vital for the development of our country that the doctrine of 'sustainable development' is adopted by us as a balancing concept.

Corruption

India has seen many corruption scandals in the past. These scandals provided us with a learning experience on how to improve the functioning of governance in the country. Under this broad topic, I have discussed how Odisha took steps in the right direction when it stated that political and bureaucratic functionaries would be mandatorily required to file their property returns with Lokayukta annually. The purpose of such disclosures was not only to help in detecting and punishing the corrupt but also to be a preventive step in curbing corruption.

With this view, I have endeavoured to collate and systematise my essays which have appeared in Economic and Political Weekly, DailyO, The Times of India, The Hindu BusinessLine, The Wire, The New Indian Express, The Financial Express, Hindustan Times, The Outlook, The Indian Express, The Telegraph, The Quint, The Print, Firstpost, ET Telecom, The Telecom, The Economic Times and Live Mint over a period of years. These essays will allow the reader to understand the various forces which were at play in India during the pandemic years.

ACKNOWLEDGEMENTS

First and foremost, praises and thanks to God, the Almighty, for his blessings and for helping us survive this gruesome global pandemic COVID-19. These pandemic years not only took a lot from us, but also taught us valuable lessons in changing routines, relationships and values. It taught us to slow down and reflect. In this book, I have tried to articulate my understanding of various issues and how they unfolded in these past two years. My deep and sincere gratitude to our Hon'ble Vice President, Shri Venkaiah Naidu Ji and the Hon'ble Chief Minister of Odisha, Shri Naveen Patnaik Ji for taking time out of their busy schedules to write special messages for the readers of this book. Special thanks are also due to my friend and fellow parliamentarian, Shri Jairam Ramesh Ji for graciously agreeing to write the Foreword for this book and for all his encouraging words as always.

I am extremely grateful to my parents for their love, prayers, care and sacrifices and for educating and guiding me at every step of the way. I am also very thankful to my wife and daughters for their love, understanding, prayers and constant support to complete the book.

I would also like to extend gratitude to my team in Delhi, viz. Jameela Sahiba, Geeta Kanwar, Suhani Pandey, Paromita Roy and Anshuman Sharma who assisted me in my research work for the various essays in this book.

I thank Shri Rashmi Ranjan Panda of Kalinga Literary Festival and Shri Atul K Thakur, Columnist & Author for facilitating publication of the book. And finally, I thank all concerned at Vitasta Publishing Pvt Ltd for publishing the book.

FOREWORD

Amar Patnaik is one of the most active and engaged MPs in the Rajya Sabha. He came to Parliament after a distinguished career in the civil service and that background, expertise and experience is always reflected in both his short interventions and longer speeches in the Council of States. Belonging to a regional party, he has naturally to give primacy to issues of concern, relevance and interest to Odisha which he represents. But he has managed to cover a wider canvas as well.

Over the past two years he has also emerged as a very thoughtful analyst of and commentator on diverse public policy issues in the print media—a media that is under threat from other forms of communication but still has a distinctive importance of its own. This anthology brings together his sharp writings on variety of topics—health, education, technology, environment, economy, financial management and social welfare. They are based not only on his long years in public administration but also on what he has observed and learnt as a MP.

Amar Patnaik has spoken on many of the subjects covered in the book in Parliament and in Parliamentary committees not all of which were picked up widely at the time they were made. This volume of his mini-essays will undoubtedly help a larger audience to appreciate his contributions in the Parliamentary system since he became a part of it. They are written in simple, jargon-free language (which is not easy for an ex-bureaucrat!) but convey the message which he wishes to put across very effectively. These writings demonstrate that in addition to being a former civil servant and a serving lawmaker the author has an academic bent of mind—in the best and scholarly sense of the term. I should also add that while this is an anthology of what has appeared in different sections of the media, the writings continue to not have lost their topicality and continue to have relevance.

It has been a privilege to have been asked to write this foreword. It has been a pleasure and education to listen to Amar Patnaik—and also as a result of this book to read him also. He also belongs to rare breed of MP species—those who frequent the wonderfully rich but little used Parliament library.

—Jairam Ramesh

MP & Author

April 11, 2022

SPECIAL MESSAGE

Namasthe!

Thank you for sharing the manuscript of your upcoming book titled "Pandemic Disruptions and Odisha's Lessons in Governance".

The past couple of years have indeed tested the fortitude and resilience of humanity as countries across the world have grappled with the ravaging COVID-19 pandemic. No doubt, humanity across the world, with its sheer grit and cooperation has overcome the challenge of this deadly disease by inoculating an unprecedented percentage of the population in the world through mass vaccination programmes.

I am sure this book containing your insights into many issues that emerged in India during the pandemic will be very informative for the readers.

With best wishes,

—Venkaiah Naidu

Hon'ble Vice-President of India

28th March, 2022

SPECIAL MESSAGE

The book 'Pandemic Disruptions and Odisha's Lessons in Governance' by Dr. Amar Patnaik, Member of Parliament and former Principal Accountant General of Odisha covers a diverse set of subjects that caught public imagination and concern during the difficult pandemic times – health, education, technology, privacy, economy and Odisha's performances. His analysis of the overall Odisha model of Governance in various sectors using the 5T framework is quite appreciative including his subtle understanding of other issues.

Dr. Patnaik has also dwelled upon important issues such as data protection, data privacy as a fundamental right, artificial intelligence, the rise in mistrust in communities due to asymmetric economic and social conditions in the essays in his book.

I wish the publication of the book all success.

—Naveen Patnaik

Hon'ble Chief Minister of Odisha

CHAPTER 1

COVID 19 MANAGEMENT AND OTHER PUBLIC HEALTH CONCERNS

1.1 COVID 19 and the requirement to invest in equitable public health systems

India's public health system has struggled to cope with the COVID-19 crisis. Even before the pandemic, India's public health infrastructure was inadequate with only 0.55 beds per 1,000 population, while out-of-pocket expenditure was pushing almost 63 million people back into poverty, as a large number of healthcare positions lie vacant across the country. Faced with a growing disease burden, India's public health system is in dire need of investment and the COVID-19 crisis is the perfect opportunity to back this policy decision with political will.

Early in the lockdown, India had relative control over curbing the potential spread of COVID-19, and may have prevented as many as five times more cases in April in a scenario without a lockdown (Dwivedi et al 2020). However, some states succeeded more than others. Among larger states, Kerala and Odisha performed relatively better for varying reasons like an efficient public health system and timely response, respectively. However, as experts kept suggesting, the peak of the spread was still likely in the future, while our public health systems were already strained to full capacity. Health System's Response to the ongoing crisis has brought into focus three important arguments.

First, robust health systems like in Kerala are better placed in containing the spread and providing care to citizens. Even before COVID-19, Kerala had fared well in containing the Nipah outbreak. Had Nipah not been contained within the state, it could have become a national epidemic. Globally, too, countries with robust health systems have already flattened the curve and have started coming out of lockdowns.

Second, the COVID-19 crisis has provided a glimpse of what a full-scale public health response looks like. For instance, Odisha, which is experienced at tackling super cyclones like Amphan, has adopted a disaster management approach and mobilised resources more effectively than most states and has been more successful in containing the spread and keeping the case fatality rate low. Odisha established quarantine facilities, created more hospital beds and allocated more resources towards combating the crisis. The main governance strategy in the state has been that of decentralisation and trusting panchayats to manage the pandemic response at the village level, and converting schools and colleges into isolation centres. This strategy prevented pressures on the health systems and the healthcare workforce. In the state and even nationally, public health communication has been a continuous feature of the crisis response, with messages about personal hygiene, social distancing and public safety emerging as key topics of dissemination.

Third, India's public health system is in dire need of investment, and since we are witnessing that public health emergencies can bring down not just national but global economies, long lockdowns and emergency responses cannot be the only way to deal with them. Studies have shown that with climate change (McMichael 2015) and increased mobility of people, infectious diseases are more likely to occur in the future (Hoberg and Brooks 2015). Moreover, India is going through an epidemiological transition, implying that the disease profile of the country is diverse, which puts additional pressure on the health system. Combine a pandemic with an inadequate health system and we had a situation where Indians were predisposed to larger lockdowns in any crisis, with the poor being disproportionately affected, as has been evident in the COVID-19 crisis.

In most states, the public health infrastructure is inadequate and has struggled to cater to the health needs of the citizens, even in times of relative normalcy before the COVID-19 pandemic.

Public Health Infrastructure

Health infrastructure is the foundation to deliver an effective health system response to the delivery of health services. To prevent, manage, or cure a health condition, adequate healthcare infrastructure is essential, which includes beds, doctors, paramedics, etc. The National Health Profile 2019 (CBHI 2019) highlighted that there were 7,13,986 total government hospital beds available in India or about 0.55 beds per 1,000 population. For comparison, Sri Lanka, which is a neighbouring country with a better health system and similar Gross Domestic Product (GDP) per capita, has 3.7 beds per 1,000 population, and China, which is comparable in population size, has 4.2 beds per 1,000 population, respectively, while the World Health Organization (WHO) recommends five beds per 1,000 population.

Moreover, there are 12 states with 70% of India's population that have less than 0.55 beds per 1,000 population, namely Bihar, Jharkhand, Gujarat, Uttar Pradesh (UP), Andhra Pradesh, Chhattisgarh, Madhya Pradesh (MP), Haryana, Maharashtra, Odisha, Assam, and Manipur. States like Sikkim (2.34) fare better on this indicator, while Kerala (1.05), Delhi (1.05), and Tamil Nadu (1.1) fare moderately.

Similarly, WHO recommends one physician per 1,000 population and India fares at 0.8, while Sri Lanka fares at 1, and China at 1.8 physicians per 1,000 population. Even in trained surgical workforce, India lags way behind with seven surgeons per 1,00,000 population compared to China's 40 surgeons per 1,00,000 population. To train this highly skilled workforce, India will need to substantially improve on its 529 medical colleges, which take in about 58,756 students each year.

It is important to understand the impact the low availability of healthcare infrastructure and human resources has on the citizens. Since public facilities are inadequate, citizens frequently turn to private healthcare providers, bearing the cost of healthcare on their own. While it may be a normal practice for those who can afford it, for our poorest citizens, it may be the biggest reason that is keeping them poor.

Pushing Millions into Poverty

In India, spending on private healthcare is much higher than that on public health compared to many other countries at a similar stage of development.

More importantly, even in private spending, the share of Out-of-Pocket (OoP) expenditure is much higher. The lack of adequate public health and high OoP expenditure imposes a high financial burden on Indian households. OoP spending on health is pushing millions of Indians into poverty. A study estimated, using the National Sample Survey Office (NSSO) survey, that around 63.22 million individuals or 11.88 million households were pushed below the poverty line due to healthcare expenditure (Bhandari et al 2010). The paper also found that 6.2% of total households (6.6% in rural areas and 5% in urban areas) fell into the below poverty line (BPL) category as a result of total healthcare expenditure. Around 1.3% of total households (1.3% in rural areas and 1.2% in urban areas) fell into the BPL category as a result of expenditure on inpatient care, while 4.9% of households (5.3% in rural areas and 3.8% in urban areas) fell into the BPL category as a result of outpatient care.

Moreover, much of this impoverishment (79.3%) is due to outpatient care, which involves relatively small but more frequent payments, and only 20.7% of impoverishment is due to inpatient care. The paper also found that a higher share of this burden is borne by those living in rural areas, possibly due to transportation costs to private facilities situated in the nearest urban centres. It is important to understand how the poor finance this OoP burden. A paper by Flores et al (2008) provides some important insights into this. The paper highlights that in rural areas, borrowing is the main financial coping mechanism, financing almost 34% of OoP expenditures, whereas in urban areas, savings are the main source of funding but borrowing still accounts for 22% of health expenditure. The situation is so dire, the paper finds that increased expenditure or borrowing to finance OoP payments does not lead to contraction of other spending, but rather an inflation in overall household expenditure, indicating a permanent debt trap. It has also been documented globally that more than hospitalisation costs, recurring payments for medical supplies and pharmacy cause a bigger dent in household finances (Wagstaff and Doorslaer 2003).

One of the key goals of a health system is to protect populations from large financial risks associated with healthcare expenditures. It is imperative that India invests in its public health infrastructure. Even during times of relative normalcy, our health systems are stretched, and the poor bear the burden of poor public health by shelling out money from their pockets to seek healthcare.

India's High Disease Burden

India has what is called the "triple burden of disease," which implies that the Indian population, with around 85 lakh deaths per year, is susceptible to preventable infectious diseases, non-communicable diseases, as well as injury related ailments.

While the total share of deaths due to infectious diseases has gone down over the last couple of decades, these diseases still cause the most number of premature deaths in the country, with five of the top seven causes of premature deaths in India in this group (ICMR et al 2017). When combined causes of death and disability are studied, malnutrition and dietary risks, like anaemia, still feature as the top two causes. In the last decade, India has also witnessed a rise in non-communicable diseases (NCDs), which in the past were considered diseases of affluence or lifestyle diseases. The top three causes of death in India currently are cardiovascular conditions (heart disease), chronic obstructive pulmonary disease (COPD - lung diseases) and stroke, and these diseases also feature in the top six causes of premature deaths. In the last decade, the prevalence of asthma, diabetes, and kidney disease has also risen (ICMR et al 2017). India also faces a high number of injury-related deaths and disabilities like self-harm and road accidents. India has the world's highest number of road accidents at about five lakh annual accident cases or about 1,370 accidents per day (NCRB 2017).

Burden of disease is measured by a metric called disability-adjusted life years (DALYs), measuring the loss of years in good health because of premature death, disease, or disability. One DALY represents one lost year of healthy life. DALYs vary for different disease groups. For infectious diseases, DALYs are as high as nine-fold for diarrhoeal disease, seven-fold for lower respiratory infections and nine-fold for tuberculosis in 2016, because of higher mortality compared to years lived with disability and given that a lot of these deaths occur at younger ages. From an economic and policy point of view, DALYs are critical for an economy and imply life lived under the "burden" of morbidity, often accompanied with decreased productivity, financial burden on family members, rising health costs, and debt. In India, while accidents and injuries are spread out across the country, the other two disease groups are not as omnipresent. Communicable or infectious diseases are mostly concentrated in the poorer and less economically developed states, often categorised as the Empowered Action Group (EAG), which includes Bihar, Jharkhand, UP, Uttarakhand, MP, Chhattisgarh, Odisha, Rajasthan, and Assam. Southern states transitioned epidemiologically before northern states.

For example, the infant mortality rate in Kerala had fallen as early as the 1980s, and in the last 30 years, the burden of NCDs has risen gradually in the south. However, in the last decade, NCDs have risen across the country.

What is more important is that even neighbouring states can have vastly different disease profiles. The India State-Level Disease Burden report highlights that MP and UP, both with relatively lower levels of development indicators and a similar epidemiological transition stage, differ in disease profiles (ICMR et al 2017). UP had 50% higher disease burden from chronic obstructive pulmonary disease, 54% higher burden from tuberculosis, and 30% higher burden from diarrhoeal diseases, whereas MP had 76% higher disease burden per person from stroke. Disease outcomes cannot be seen in isolation from geographic, cultural, and economic factors. Punjab, for example, has a higher than average consumption of alcohol with 28.5% people consuming alcohol, which is one of the factors directly correlated with heart disease, and road injuries due to drunk-driving. Alcohol consumption in Himachal Pradesh for comparison is 8.9% (NDDTC 2019). India's past experience has shown that the country as a whole has been successful whenever it has worked in a mission mode: eradication of polio, keeping HIV prevalence low, and in the case of COVID-19 responding with a disaster management approach. Moreover, India's public health system is omnipresent, albeit one that underperforms.

What India needs to build on is for times of crisis as well as relative normalcy. For that, improving on service delivery, training workforce, and financing public health are extremely critical. Studies have suggested that despite its omnipresence,

India's public health system is underutilised, mainly due to trust issues and perceived higher quality in private clinics, suggesting that there are issues in the quality of care provided at the public health facilities.

Public Health Services

Reforming a health system is a mid to long-term task and has been challenging for governments around the world. Different countries have adopted varying strategies to reform their health systems as per local contexts and needs. However, there are a couple of widely-used frameworks that can be referred to while planning for a health system reform. One of the most popular frameworks is the WHO Building Blocks framework, which lists six building blocks for an effective health system: service delivery; health workforce; information; medical products, vaccines and technologies; financing and leadership/ governance (WHO 2007).

Another popular framework is the "Control Knobs Model" of health system reform, which prioritises financing, payments, organisation, regulation, and persuasion as "knobs" that the government can manipulate to achieve a desired health system (Roberts et al 2004). In both models, there are key common intermediate variables that explain the pathway to achieving desired system goals. These are access to facilities, equity through financial risk protection, quality of health services, and affordability of health costs.

Access to Facilities

Access to healthcare must include access to both infrastructure as well as human resources for health. To achieve an effective primary and tertiary-care infrastructure, a workable strategy could be to build on what India currently has. India has a large network of primary health centres; however, they are often underfunded, ill-equipped and the staff is undertrained or even absent. Moreover, there are a large number of healthcare positions that lie vacant. Tertiary care in India is also often considered inadequate by WHO recommended standards and is in dire need of an upgrade. Overall, we need to upgrade the capacity of both the infrastructure and human resources to a minimum standard, which could be WHO prescribed standards or comparative standards of a similar better-performing country.

Various reports have put the available human resources for health at 8 to 11 human resources per 10,000 population as against the WHO prescribed figure of 25 to 26 per 10,000. According to one estimate, the number of allopathic doctors, nurses, and midwives combined (11.9 per 10,000 people) was about half the WHO benchmark of 25.4 workers per 10,000 population (Rao et al 2011).

Moreover, these resources are unequally distributed across the country. In northern and central states, which happen to be the poorest regions of the country, the number of health workers is even lower. There is a wide geographical and urban–rural variation too, as almost 69% of India's population in villages have access to only about 26% of the country's doctors. Among these, the share of doctors in the private sector is considerably higher than those in the public health sector. To redistribute a high number of doctors to the rural areas is a gargantuan task. However, it is something that has been achieved before, most notably in Turkey, which successfully introduced health system changes and provided its citizens with the right to health to achieve universal health coverage, and addressed inequities in health service access and health outcomes (Atun et al 2013). For India, Odisha's success in swiftly signing the memorandum of understanding and getting into public–private partnership agreements with private sector healthcare can be replicated, especially in states where the public health system is far from providing adequate healthcare immediately. The vast network of private hospitals, clinics and other doctors and paramedics need to be effectively collaborated with while addressing adequacy to provide access to healthcare.

Moreover, investing in centres of healthcare and healthcare training will be a prudent investment for India. Not only will more health training cater to the deficiency of medical human resources across the country, it will also provide critical care at places where those centres are established. Centres like All India Institute of Medical Sciences (AIIMS), which India prides itself in, are indeed a need at a much lower level. India could look at district-level plans for high-quality healthcare and healthcare training centres. Investing in a high-quality health care and training centre in a cluster of three to four districts could be a strategic long-term investment and should be prioritised. Moreover, certain district-level hospitals could also be remodelled to work as district-level health and wellness centres to provide more holistic healthcare at the district level.

Equity through financial risk protection

Equity in the health system should ensure that healthcare costs do not become a financial burden on the poor and the economically disadvantaged, as it is at present. For the last 15 years or so, there has been an increased focus on state-sponsored public health insurance. With this view, the Rashtriya Swasthya Bima Yojana (RSBY), now Pradhan Mantri Swasthya Suraksha Yojana (PMSSY) was launched. The scheme was also seen as a move towards universal health insurance coverage. More recently, the PMJAY scheme aims to cover the bottom 40% of the population, based on the socio-economic caste census, with an insurance cover-age of up to Rs 5 lakh for hospitalisation.

However, studies have shown ineffective utilisation of national and state-sponsored insurance schemes. In the most recent and comprehensive study, it was found that only a maximum of 38% of those enrolled under state health insurance utilised the public health facilities (Prinja et al 2019). The study also found that the mean OoP expenditures for outpatient care among the insured and uninsured were `961 ($16) and `840 ($14), and `32,573 ($543) and `24,788 ($413) for an episode of hospitalisation, respectively. The most alarming finding of the study was that catastrophic health expenditure among the insured and the uninsured was almost similar at 28% and 26%, respectively, with that among the insured marginally higher. Indian poor are not protected against financial strains in times of healthcare needs and the OoP expenditure remains high.

However, it is not to say that utilisation of the public health system always yields undesired results. In terms of maternal health indicators and improving institutional deliveries, the public sector has led the way and provided inexpensive and accessible health services (Prinja et al 2012).

The public sector has the ability to provide cost-effective services that are utilised by the citizens. Even if the public sector cannot provide all services in a cost-effective manner, it can definitely cater to the poor, with basic services and reduce catastrophic expenditure on health. Universal insurance or universal public healthcare is much desired by most policymakers. However, till the time we reach that stage in terms of state finance and the health system's capacity, the public sector can compete with the private sector to provide quality services.

An example of moving towards universal health coverage is the Biju Swasthya Kalyan Yojana (BSKY) in Odisha, which provides coverage for both above poverty line (APL) and BPL populations in the state, unlike the Ayushman Bharat Scheme, which only covers BPL households. Under the scheme, besides free healthcare services at government healthcare institutions up to district headquarters hospital level, additional facility of free healthcare beyond district headquarters hospital level, through annual health coverage of Rs 5 lakh per annum per family and Rs 7 lakh per annum for women members of the family is also provided. This scheme also serves all currently enrolled Biju Krushak Kalyan Yojana cardholders, RSBY cardholders, BPL cardholders and Antyodaya Anna Yojana (AAY) cardholders and families with annual income below `50,000 in rural areas and below`60,000 in urban areas. The BSKY covers the target population even at the primary-care level by providing free health services in state government healthcare facilities starting from sub-centre level up to the district headquarters hospital level through a network of Swasthya Mitras (health buddies) working as point of care query response executives. Besides public hospitals, 208 private hospitals are also empanelled under the scheme and the claim settlement is provided by insurance companies. Quality of health services: Quality in healthcare is achieved through public satisfaction of services provided at the public health facilities. Quality of service delivery is an essential component of building trust with the citizens and improving utilisation of public health facilities.

The Mohalla clinics in Delhi are a good example of improving service quality and building trust and reliance with citizens. A study highlighted that a key reason for higher utilisation of Mohalla clinics was less waiting time at clinics, increased interaction time with the doctor, perceived performance of doctor, and effectiveness of treatment (Agrawal et al 2020). The study also pointed out that similar reasons motivated the users to return to the facility to seek healthcare. Other state governments could adopt these lessons and improve the service quality at public health centres. Of course, there is no substitute for high-quality tertiary care that can save lives and a network of multi-specialty tertiary care centres are a need across the country, which, barring some elite medical institutions, is restricted to big private hospitals around the country.

Affordability of health costs

Affordability ensures that not just primary but tertiary care is also not placing a catastrophic burden on citizens. However, affordability is not only about an inexpensive public health sector. In the presence of a large private health sector, the public health sector needs to provide good-quality care to compete and provide similar satisfaction as private facilities. This would ensure competition and reduce prices even in the private sector.

Additionally, there is a need to regulate prices of healthcare costs and drugs. Prices of private healthcare can be as high as six to eight times that of public facilities (NSSO 2019). These costs include only inpatient costs; however, the costs for pharmacy and drugs are also much higher compared to medicines at public facilities and pharmacies. Affordability is not a stand-alone argument and needs to be seen with the whole function of a public health system. To reduce high costs of tertiary care, it is imperative that a strong primary-care network exists across the country that can diagnose and refer disease early. An effective primary-care system can also prevent a lot of conditions becoming adverse. Most effective health systems, like Japan, prioritise prevention of disease as a public health strategy. Since most health conditions, infectious or non-communicable, are preventable, this strategy keeps the burden on the health system low and minimises DALYs.

Conclusion

State-specific prevention strategies require customising health infrastructure as well as tailoring the technical capacity of human resources. In UP, for instance, front-line health workers need training support on infectious disease control and modules of how to navigate socio-cultural gatekeepers to enable behaviour change at the community level. Similarly, in Punjab, an effective outreach would require motivating families and individuals to moderate the consumption of alcohol and adopt healthier diets. This level of outreach requires a dynamic primary healthcare system that is adept at responding to local needs with local contexts, and utilises technology to deliver quality of care at primary, secondary and tertiary care centres. To achieve an accessible, equitable, quality, and affordable health system, government financing is indispensable. However, India does not spend as much as most public health literature would recommend. The WHO recommends spending 6% of the GDP on health. In 2020, India budgeted to spend about 1% of its GDP on healthcare.

To invest in upgrading the number and capacity of human resources and modernising infrastructure, public health will require a higher priority in terms of financing. Currently, health does not feature as priority expenditure in our national budget. The type of reform our health system needs will require massive investments from our national budgets and a strong political will at the national as well as state levels. Advocating for increased health expenditure as a percentage of national budgets is the first step towards realising an effective public health system. The government health expenditure (GHE) per person per year in India is only Rs 1,108, which comes to Rs 3 per day. States have started prioritising increased health spending within their annual budgets, with Delhi as a notable example. Other states like Mizoram and Sikkim have better functioning public health systems, which is directly correlated with their high per capita expenditure on public health, at `5,862 and `5,126, respectively (MoHFW 2017). Larger states like Odisha have started investing in public health with a multi-pronged approach to investment. Already, plans for an AIIMS-like centre are underway and cancer treatment facilities along with medical colleges in each district have been planned for the state. There is much to learn from experiences of different states as well, as India is vast and diverse and so are the health needs and strategies of its states. What was critical during the COVID-19 crisis is that we prioritise health, not just in policy but also with political will. Increasing investment in health will surely compromise spending on other sectors and may be politically tricky. However, with the COVID-19 pandemic, there will not be a safer opportunity than right now to show political will and make reformative investments in our public health system, which could directly lead to millions of our citizens being healthier and at less financial risk.

1.2 New social order post the lockdown

Within four weeks, India has come to adjust with normalcy that restrains us from going to work, socialise with friends, engage in religious and cultural activities and most importantly, interact freely with the outside world.

This rigorous implementation of social distancing and physical quarantine could establish a new normal for social interactions in communities and societies in future, which could be extremely tech-driven, digital and contactless.

Role of social media

Consequently, some pertinent questions arise for sociologists and policy practitioners. Despite the physical isolation, will the much-vaunted social cohesion remain intact in Indian communities? Will social restraint increase or decrease social capital?

According to the sociologist Robert Putnam, relationships and interactions based on trust beget social bonding, which in turn fosters 'social capital'. This social capital acts as a glue to bind communities and societies together, leading to what is commonly called 'social cohesion'. There are two kinds of social capital—bonding which is horizontal and bridging that is vertical. The former refers to interactions and relationships within the community or society while the latter refers to the trust relationship between the individual or the community and the leaders or the government. Bonding social capital increases when individuals adopt the norms of reciprocity and trustworthiness through social networking. This would include both physical and non-physical interactions. While India's social fabric has traditionally been characterised by the implicit trust within the community, which is a source of Joseph Nye's 'soft power', such trust is somewhat weak when it comes to the relationship between the individual and the government.

A behavioural change at the sub-conscious level is afoot, while individuals accept the new routine of social distancing. It has forced people to learn to be self-contained in their gregarious as well as material needs, leading to more time for families, parents and hobbies. So, an increase in intra-family bonding is expected. But the fear is that this could also lead to people decreasing their dependence on others outside the family. But here, interestingly, social media has been a game-changer. Social media groups on WhatsApp, Facebook, TikTok and Instagram, and outreach through them have increased manifold during the time of the lockdown and has, in fact, made the community more tightly knit. Thus, in effect, the bonding social capital within the community may have increased during the lockdown and may show similar trend even afterwards.

Shift in power

The major source of mistrust within Indian communities has been the asymmetries in economic and social power. However, this pandemic has been a great leveller. People realise that even the most powerful and the rich North couldn't insulate themselves against the disease. At a microscopic level, the same logic pans out at the level of communities too, leading to a notional and perceived reduction in the usual economic and social power asymmetries that exist amongst communities in India. People realise that the disease doesn't distinguish between the higher and the lower castes. To this extent, this pandemic is very different from an economic recession or a natural disaster because in the latter cases, the rich and the higher caste people invariably escape the worst while it is the poor who lose much in terms of life and livelihood.

When it comes to the bridging social capital, the success of 'Janata Curfew' followed by the 21-day lockdown (later extended by 19 days) has shown that a call for collective action by the government is being adhered to and respected by the majority of 1.3 billion Indians. The people have displayed complete trust in what their local, state or central governments have been saying and doing, viz. may it be observing the preventive practices of frequent hand washing or wearing masks and even a very difficult and novel institutional mechanism for most, called social distancing.

A fresh paradigm

These are evidence of a strong and evolving bridging social capital based on trust and reciprocity between the community/ society with the government which, quite frankly, most of us had never seen in the actual display. Even in the non-government sector, the management has adapted to trust the remotely working employees under the work-from-home protocol. What has essentially happened is that community ownership over governmental or organisational action, which was largely weak in India, has suddenly become very robust.

One finds there is a wave of support and humanity towards the army of health, sanitation, municipal and police professionals fighting the virus at the forefront. People have started valuing their services, which they had earlier taken for granted. The sense of civic duty and citizenship amongst most people has deepened. Many informal chains have mushroomed reaching out to families in need like the elderly and poor jobless migrant workers in need of food and shelter.

Thus, it appeared that post lockdown, a new social order based on social distancing would emerge that, instead of weakening the Indian social fabric, would strengthen both the bonding and bridging social capital leading to increased societal cohesion and resilience. But whether it would sustain before mounting economic losses is something to be watched.

1.3 Pressing priority for rapid and smart tests

The world seems to finally be entering the conclusive phase of battling the coronavirus. We have collectively learnt and improved a lot along the way, as evidenced by the sharp drop-in mortality rates despite high rates of hospitalisation in most countries. We also have multiple vaccine candidates with very high claims of efficacy, applying for emergency use authorisations with regulators globally, including in India. Countries have started approving the use of these vaccines as well, and some like the UK have already launched mass vaccination campaigns. Two vaccine candidates have been approved in India. Following this strategy, India launched the world's largest vaccination drive on January 16, 2021. The inoculation drive entered its third phase on April 1, 2021, with people over the age of 45 and above eligible for vaccination.

However, as optimistic as the times to come looked, it was crucial that we did not take our focus off the task at hand — minimising the spread of the infection by rigorous testing and contact tracing. Instead of letting our guard down, now was the time for the country to increase vigil and consolidate all the gains that we have achieved thus far. Our premier scientific research institution, the ICMR, had gained a lot more information and experience with the novel coronavirus and expecting clearer and more decisive strategies is natural. Already several states were leading by examples and offering critical lessons to formulate strategies for the country.

Odisha, for instance, had exceeded expectations in its management of the pandemic considering all the odds that were stacked against it. The state powered through the challenges of infrastructure inadequacy, existing health burden and also survived destructions brought by Cyclone Amphan solely because of the state government's resolve and timely action. The administration followed a scientific and data-driven decision-making process to keep the virus under check within the region. They ensured equity and accessibility of testing, backed by a smart tracing strategy to keep check on the spread of the virus. In early December, the cost of RT-PCR tests at private labs were capped at Rs 400 in the state, the lowest in India, to make testing for COVID-19 vastly more accessible and affordable. This was done keeping the local context in mind — that a large population of the state was economically vulnerable and had one of the lowest per capita earnings in the country. Additionally, to ensure that people can get themselves tested without having to travel afar, in a short span of time, more than 55 COVID-19 testing labs had been operationalised in the state.

These steps taken by the state of Odisha yielded some very positive results. From nearly 1,500 cases daily in the first week of November 2020, the numbers reduced by more than two-thirds to less than 400 in just the month that followed. This was while the number of daily tests conducted had remained stable, despite the sharp fall in positivity. Such a remarkable testing strategy had also been well complemented by equally important measures such as door-to-door health screening so as to be able to actively scout for those with symptoms. Keeping in view the above, it was not surprising that Odisha was among the lower rates of test positivity as well as fatality among states in India. Odisha paved the way for the need to emulate this successful model of testing and tracing at a national scale.

With the arrival of vaccines for COVID-19, the importance of putting in place a smart testing and tracing strategy for the entire country had gone up manifold, contrary to popular perceptions. Despite best efforts from all stakeholders, it took several months to reach the critical mass of population necessary to break the chain of transmission under a national vaccination strategy, especially since most vaccines required the initial dose to be followed up with a second dose after an interval of three to four weeks. Moreover, there were groups which were being prioritised (healthcare workers, frontline workers, persons above age of 50 and those below 50 with associated comorbidities) and a graded plan of access was drawn up. Given India's sheer population size, relatively underdeveloped infrastructure (like, existing cold chain systems) as well as the logistical considerations associated with different vaccine candidates, it proved to be a challenge to cover a majority of the population immediately. At this time, tools like testing and tracing were continued to be leveraged, especially among populations that did not feature in the priority order. This is not the time for complacency.

It is evident from Haryana's home minister Anil Vij's case that testing will continue to occupy centre-stage even after the vaccine is administered. Shortly after receiving the first dose of Bharat Biotech's Covaxin trial vaccine, he announced that he had tested positive. This does not sufficiently allude to the low efficacy or utility of the vaccine, given that this was a double-blinded trial where he may have been administered with a placebo. By his own admission, he had not received the booster dose of the vaccine, which was a necessary component. But fact remains that it is entirely possible to get infected in the interval between the two doses since the body does not develop sufficient immunity and testing in the interim is the only way to detect such cases.

Similarly, for drawing up a national vaccination strategy, it is crucial to gauge the spread of the virus and check for those with antibodies through previous infection to further filter the prioritisation list and reserve the initial set of vaccines for those in need of higher protection. Despite having an impressive indigenous vaccine manufacturing capacity, there are several limitations which will hinder the universal coverage of the vaccine for a substantial amount of time. It is important that the country and all institutions spearheading the response against the pandemic explores a smart testing and tracing roadmap, alongside designing strategies for vaccination.

1.4 Scripting a billion vaccinations

As India had successfully started its vaccination drive, with more than two million inoculated, there lies a promise of better years ahead. However, the fight against Covid-19 is far from over, and for the vaccination drive to be successful on a large scale, it is essential to do a long-term risk analysis of the various challenges that can arise in the course of vaccine delivery. Umpteen number of things could go wrong during the process and, as such, it is essential that a detailed vaccination programme is ideated upon before implementation. Over the years, India has put in considerable effort to make itself the vaccine manufacturer hub of the world and, as such, vaccine manufacturing will not be an issue in the long run to meet domestic demand. The main problems with the Covid-19 vaccine in the near term will however remain in terms of dealing with infrastructure woes, trained manpower, efficacy, vaccine disinformation and cost of the vaccines.

Trained manpower

A large number of trained manpower will also be needed in the vaccination process, especially for the elderly. As most of these are two-dose vaccines, it needs to ensure that every person gets two doses of the same vaccine. This will happen only with trained manpower is at hand. Right now, the vaccination is being done in controlled settings, to healthcare workers. Real problems could start when mass vaccinations commence to the public at large. (The article was written on Feb 04, 2021.)

Data, testing and tracing

Data is another sore point in the current testing and tracing scenario. If the government is not forthcoming with accurate data, it will create obstacles during the vaccination process. Antigen tests need to be reported accurately so that an informed decision can be taken during vaccination.

If accurate data is not reported on who has been previously infected or not, it will create problems during the vaccination process, as the science is not yet precise on whether infected people can be vaccinated.

There should be an equally efficacious regime for the collection of data relating to adverse effects of the vaccines administered in different age groups where India's track record has not been very inspiring.

Storage and transport

Two of the most efficacious vaccines from Pfizer and Moderna require ultra-high cold storage facilities, and India has very little of those. Moreover, according to the Comptroller and Auditor General (CAG) report from 2017, many States lack not just ultra-high cold storage facilities for vaccines but also have no deep freezers, ice-lined refrigerators (ILR), and vaccine carriers to maintain the vaccines at the prescribed range of temperature.

The government needs to quickly ramp up the procurement of cold-chain storage systems; else, it will not be able to meet the considerable demand for vaccination in the country.

A key driver during previous vaccination programmes has been the high level of trust entrusted into the process by the public. However, if the current process continues to be opaque, it will not be easy in the long run to get people vaccinated.

With the rise of social media apps, it will not take long to spread fake news about the vaccine and the vaccination process.

Bust myths, misinformation

The rise of anti-vaxxers has been a perplexing dilemma in modern societies, and it is crucial that the government takes the lead in busting myths and misinformation around vaccines and increase awareness on the adoption of vaccines and their benefits. We are already seeing hesitancy among healthcare workers in receiving the vaccines due to unclear data and concerns over safety and efficacy of the vaccines.

Hence, it is imperative that the government puts the data of all vaccine candidates on trial in India in public domain to be independently verified by domain experts. Moreover, political leaders should vaccinate themselves on live television to inspire confidence among the citizens and remove any doubts about the vaccine's efficacy.

The government had the foresight to establish a Vaccination Task Force even in August, 2021 which dealt with all issues including vaccine production, tracking and storage. State governments also established special task forces to figure out the logistical challenges in delivering the vaccines to the last mile. As different vaccine candidates are under consideration in India, the government would be well-advised to choose those which are more effective in producing an immune response and not those that are most cost-effective or cheaper.

Moreover, the government should also try not to differentiate between geographies by introducing different vaccines at different places. Citizens should have multiple options to choose from, and the government should not decide it for them. If the vaccination is well-planned and done collaboratively, it could be a remarkable case study for the future.

1.5 Balancing domestic COVID 19 vaccine needs vis a vis global demand

India's fight against the COVID-19 virus-induced pandemic has been globally applauded. Beginning September 2020, the coronavirus cases in India saw a steady decline. With a steady dip in the cases and the rollout of the first phase of India's vaccination programme in January 2021, it appeared that the end was near. However, there has been a sharp uptick in coronavirus cases in March 2021. India recorded 72,108 confirmed cases of coronavirus disease on March 31st, 2021- the highest ever surge in daily cases since October 11, 2020. Due to the nature of the spread of this virus, it is amply clear that the way out of the pandemic is through mass vaccination. The IMF and World Bank have said, "No one is safe until everyone is safe." The WHO has exhorted the member countries to vaccinate its health care workers and older people within the first 100 days of 2021. Following this strategy, India launched the world's largest vaccination drive on January 16, 2021. The inoculation drive had entered its third phase on April 1, 2021, with people over the age of 45 and above eligible for vaccination.

Global equity concerns

Certainly, mass vaccination is the way to beat the pandemic, but it must go hand in hand with equitable distribution of the vaccines. There has been a dominance of the high-income countries in the global vaccination drive. It has been over three months since the high-income countries started their vaccinations but there are still frontline workers in poor countries who have not received a single dose of the vaccine. Glaring vaccination inequities have surfaced within and among countries.

As of March 30, 2021, the US has vaccinated about 44 people per 100 population whereas its neighbour Canada has inoculated only 14 people per 100 population. Similar inequities in the vaccine's distribution exist among the countries of Asia, Europe and South America.

For example, while India has vaccinated about 5 people per 100 population, China has inoculated about 8 people per 100 population. As many countries face the fresh onslaught of the third wave of infection because of mutants of the COVID-19 virus, there needs to be an equitable distribution of the vaccine among and within countries.

However there are challenges. While global equity concerns are acknowledged, can it trump a country's own domestic vaccine equity concerns? The latter is very difficult to sustain politically and socially too. The murmurs can already be felt in India. While the entire world has acknowledged India's humane role in supplying vaccine to about 78 countries in the world, which has cemented its role as a global leader, some opposition parties are questioning if this was being done at the cost of poor Indians who have limited access to the vaccine.

India's domestic vaccine equity

India aimed to inoculate about 30 crores of people by the end of July 2021 with a target of 70 lakhs vaccinations daily. As of March 31, 2021, the daily vaccinations stood at about 21 lakhs while the total vaccinations were 6.5 crores. The first phase saw the frontline workers being vaccinated while in the second phase people over the age of 60 or people over the age of 45 with co-morbidities were eligible beneficiaries. The third phase then covered all above 45 years of age.

India's pulse polio immunisation effort has been applauded globally. Even though the scale of the polio vaccination was relatively limited, the lessons from the past have enabled the push for equitable distribution of vaccines. The government has leveraged its institutional networks in the form of ASHA workers, Panchayati Raj institutions and Women's Self Help Groups (SHG) to mobilise awareness at the grassroots. However, the current challenge is much more difficult as it is a highly transmissible disease and everyone has to be vaccinated, not just a target group.

The coronavirus pandemic has had a devastating effect on the Indian economy. The price cap of Rs. 250 in private hospitals and the vaccination being free of cost in government hospitals has ensured that the economic burden of vaccination on individuals is kept to a minimum.

This has enabled individuals from economically weaker sections of the society to get vaccinated. However, barriers in the form of myths surrounding the vaccination, slower rate of vaccination as compared to global standards and availability of vaccines in topographically challenging locations persist. Further, there is an urgent need to open the vaccination across ages in the states like Maharashtra, Punjab which are currently reeling under the third wave of the pandemic.

The vision of equitable distribution of vaccine would falter if it does not account for people with lesser privileges. Irrespective of their age, individuals who cannot work from home or adhere to COVID appropriate behaviour due to the nature of their trade may act as spreaders. It is imperative that the criterion of age is not seen as the sole benchmark for vaccination.

This would only be possible through a granular data-driven approach. This would further safeguard vaccine equity for the vulnerable living in the urban and rural areas. The technical capacity of the urban and rural local bodies across the country should be strengthened to get a complete picture of the vaccinations in their area.

With the sharp spike in cases in March 2021 across the country, it is important to adhere to the principles of smart testing, treatment, tracing, and COVID appropriate behaviour which had helped us tide over the first wave. The government has been cognizant to impress upon the various state governments the need to bolster their health infrastructure in terms of ramping the testing facilities, availability of oxygen, and availability of beds.

The second wave of the pandemic could only be mitigated through a combination of equitable distribution of vaccines along with the protocols which have been honed over the last 15 months.

1.6 National Vaccination Programme—Smart testing and tracing

After a long battle, the world appears to lastly be getting into the conclusive section of battling the coronavirus. We have now collectively learnt and improved so much alongside the way in which, as evidenced by the sharp drop in mortality charges regardless of increased charges of hospitalisation in most international locations. We even have a number of vaccine candidates with very excessive claims of efficacy, making use of for emergency use authorisations with regulators globally, together with in India. Nations have begun approving using these vaccines as well and a few like the UK have already launched mass vaccination campaigns.

Nevertheless, as optimistic as the occasions for the virus to reemerge could seem, it is essential not to take the focus off the task at hand, in minimising the unfolding of the virus by rigorous testing and contact tracing. As a substitute of letting our guard down, now could be the time for the nation to extend vigil and consolidate all of the gains we've achieved to date. Our premier scientific analysis establishment, the ICMR, has gained much more data and expertise with the novel coronavirus and anticipating clearer and extra decisive methods is untainted. Already a number of states are observed by instance and providing vital classes to formulate methods for the nation. Odisha, as an illustration, has exceeded expectations in its administration of the pandemic, contemplating all the percentages that have been stacked towards it. The administration adopted a scientific approach making it a mission to maintain the virus below test throughout the area. They ensured fairness and accessibility of testing, backed by a sensible tracing technique to conduct tests on the unfolding of the virus. In early December, 2020, the cost of RT-PCR tests at private labs was capped at Rs 400 in the state, the lowest in India, to make testing for COVID-19 vastly more accessible and affordable. This was done keeping the local context in mind—that a large population of the state is economically vulnerable and has one of the lowest per capita earnings in the country. Additionally, to ensure that people can get themselves tested without having to travel afar, in the last nine months, more than 55 Covid-19 testing labs have been operationalised within the state.

These steps have yielded some constructive outcomes already. From almost 1,500 cases day on day within the first week of November, 2020, the numbers have decreased to lower than 400 in simply the month since. That is, whereas the variety of day on day tests performed has remained steady, regardless of the sharp fall in positivity.

Such an outstanding testing technique has additionally been nicely complemented by equally essential measures akin to door to door well being screening, in order to have the ability to actively scout for these with signs. Retaining this in view, it isn't surprising that Odisha has among the many decreased charges of checked positivity in addition to fatality amongst states in India. There is now a need to emulate this profitable model of testing and tracing at a nationwide scale.

With the arrival of vaccines for Covid-19, the significance of putting in a sensible testing and tracing technique for the whole nation has gone up manifold, as opposed to common perceptions.

Regardless of the finest efforts from all stakeholders, it would take a number of months to achieve the vital mass of inhabitants mandatory to interrupt the chain of transmission below a nationwide vaccination technique, particularly since most vaccines require the preliminary dose to be adopted up with a second dose after an interval of three to four weeks. Furthermore, there are teams that are being prioritised namely, healthcare employees, frontline employees, individuals above age of fifty and people under 50 with related comorbidities and a graded plan of entry should be drawn up.

Given India's population dimension in terms of sheer numbers, comparatively underdeveloped infrastructure (like, existing cold chain systems) in addition to the logistical concerns related to totally different vaccine candidates, it might be shown to be a problem to cover a majority of the inhabitants instantly. Right now, tools like testing must proceed to be leveraged, particularly amongst populations that don't function within the precedence order. This is not the time for complacency, in any respect.

For drawing up a nationwide vaccination technique, it is essential to gauge the unfolding of the virus and test for these with antibodies by way of an earlier infection, to additionally filter the prioritisation checklist and reserve the preliminary set of vaccines for those in want of priority safety. Regardless of having a formidable indigenous vaccine manufacturing capability, there are a number of limitations which can hinder the common protection of the vaccine for a considerable period of time.

It is essential that the nation and all establishments spearheading the response towards the pandemic discover a sensible testing and tracing roadmap, alongside designing methods for vaccination.

1.7 Vaccine distribution the next big challenge

Whenever we have a shortage in any essential item (goods or services), we tend to have a riot-like situation due to the size of our population. Given the number of vaccine doses required vis-a-vis the number manufactured and the miniscule percentage of people who have been inoculated so far, there is a real chance of this happening, particularly in rural areas. There are two aspects in this, viz. production (supply) and distribution.

Increasing supply

As regards enhancing production, the government's recent announcement that 216 crore doses would be available between August-December, 2021 would certainly come as a relief to all. However, what does the country do until then?

Waiver of IPR restrictions so that domestic manufacturers can produce the generic vaccine will be hard and time-consuming as it requires unanimous consensus from all WTO members. Hence, it might not be very useful to tackle the immediate and short-term supply crunch but would be valuable to increase supplies in the future.

As regards vaccines approved by the drug regulator and available in the country, the Russian vaccine Sputnik V, recently approved for emergency usage in the country, is the only one in addition to Covishield and Covaxin. The vaccine candidates of Biological E, Zydus Cadila and Gennova (mRNA) and Bharat Biotech's nasal vaccine are in various stages of clinical trials. The SII's Novovax is still in clinical trials and is likely to enter the markets only by September. The international vaccine manufacturers Pfizer, Moderna and Johnson & Johnson (single dose), who are yet to be approved by the drug controller, have stated that they can supply only in the third quarter of this year if they are assured faster regulatory clearances and freedom on pricing and exports. However, the silver lining is that the government has now clarified that any vaccine approved by the WHO and FDA, US, can be imported and administered in India.

Thus, in the immediate term, the only way to increase supply is through global vaccine imports. Multiple states including Odisha, Delhi, Rajasthan, Maharashtra and Uttar Pradesh have decided to float global tenders, which will allow them to bridge the shortage in central supply. Looking at the world market for vaccines, Pfizer plans to ramp up its manufacturing to produce 250 crore doses by the end of 2021, Moderna planned to facilitate 70 crore doses in 2021 and J&J targets manufacturing 100 crore doses by the end of 2021. However, import of these vaccines would be heavily dependent upon the real possibility of export bans by the respective countries as we hear the WHO expressing concern that rich countries have now started vaccinating children two years and above whereas several nations have not even administered the first dose to their frontline Covid warriors. Hence, these global tenders floated by the states may not bear much fruit as the vaccine manufacturers globally are limited and armed with patent rights.

Way forward to augment supplies in the immediate run

Diversifying domestic production is the need of the hour. Since Covaxin is an indigenously produced vaccine, the Indian government can allow other domestic manufacturers to produce it by waiving patent rights. The government can also use the compulsory licensing mechanism under Section 92 of the Patent Act as well as the WTO's TRIPS regime to allow domestic manufactures to also produce vaccines without fear of IPR violations. However, this may also take time as vaccine manufacture is a complicated process involving transfer of know-how as well. It is also important that the Central government quickly authorises emergency usage of vaccines that have already undergone rigorous trials in developed nations and have high efficacy. It will also increase vaccine competition and the consumers will have the option to choose from multiple vaccines, which in turn will help bring down prices and break possible monopolies. All this however is without prejudice to the fact that since the numbers of vaccine manufacturers are almost the same, they may still form a cartel thus defeating the purpose of the global tender. (The above Article was written on May 24, 2021.)

Distribution challenges

The next issue is the challenges in distribution of vaccines in rural areas. So far India has vaccinated its people mostly in cities. When it comes to rural areas, infrastructure as well as personnel issues have to be addressed in order to ensure that the vaccine administration regime complies with Covid protocol. Failure would lead to vaccine riots since people by now have gathered knowledge that vaccines are the only panacea. Another issue would be the lack of internet facility besides low tele-density (40-60%) without which logging into the COWIN app would not be possible, failing which vaccines would be denied to them. Last-mile delivery itself could be another huge, intractable bottleneck.

Conclusion

As the Covid-19 strain mutates, the government needs to prepare for a scenario where there is a need for booster shots targeting the emerging variants almost every year. Hence, it is important to build a supply chain of vaccines in the country that is resilient in the long term. If India is to vaccinate its population every year, then our demand would be the largest in the world, which itself should be a very attractive proposition for any global manufacturer.

India must also carefully calibrate its import policy to develop the correct incentives for global manufacturers to supply their vaccines in the country. To begin with, we must not ask every state to get into a contract with manufacturers separately as we may not be able to leverage placing large orders, which is an advantage for India considering our large population. The Centre must bulk buy vaccines, which will give it the negotiating power in the global market, and then distribute them amongst the states that can focus on last-mile delivery to each citizen.

1.8 TRIPS waiver and transfer of know-how

Quick vaccination against COVID 19 is the only hope in ending the global pandemic which has claimed more than 3.4 million lives so far. A hindrance to mass production of vaccines is the intellectual property rights enjoyed by their manufacturers under the WTO's Trade-related Intellectual Property Rights (TRIPS) regime. Big pharma industries are not in favour of sharing the rights and know-how needed to produce vaccines, citing intellectual property pilferage concerns. South Africa and India proposed in the October 2020 meeting of the World Trade Organization that a waiver of these patent rights would permit pharmaceutical manufacturers across the globe to manufacture vaccines using the same patented formula without fear of being legally prosecuted for intellectual property infringement. This will help meet the imminent global demand for vaccines, treatments, and other equipment.

Waiver to enhance production and supply of vaccines

Globally, the annual vaccine production has fluctuated between 3.5 – 5.5 billion doses. The onslaught of the Covid-19 induced pandemic has brought to fore a formidable challenge for the vaccine producers. It was estimated that by the end of 2021, the global vaccine demand would be at 14 billion requiring the many fold expansion of the capacity on May 25, 2021. In India, we would need about 168 crore (to vaccinate 60% only) doses against which the production capacity is 7.6 crore doses which is planned to be augmented to 13 crore doses. But even with this increased capacity, it will take 13 months to cover the entire population – a timeframe we do not have the luxury of enjoying (Written on May 25, 2021).

Given the already escalating current vaccine shortage in India which has to vaccinate its 1.40 billion population not with just one dose, but two doses in most vaccine types and not just once this year, but may be every year thereafter and besides, most of Africa has to be vaccinated as well, hence, timely and affordable vaccine would continue to be a global concern until everyone has been vaccinated. In order to meet such humongous global demand, there is utmost necessity to quickly ramp up the manufacture and supply lines. Failure to do so may result in continuing and sometime more virulent forms/strains of the virus due to potential to mutate multiple times.

There are some ill-conceived criticisms that relaxation of TRIPS regulations might affect vaccine quality. Relaxation of intellectual property rights of the vaccines is unrelated with its quality. The World Health Organization (WHO) runs a Covid-19 pre-qualification program to ascertain the quality of vaccines, where producers are required to submit their products for thorough assessment. This is like a filtration process where vaccines that do not pre-qualify for the WHO program are kept out of programs like Covax which aspire for vaccine equity especially in economically weaker nations. Besides, new on-site quality assurance mechanisms can also be introduced. The United States of America has heeded to global call and supported a temporary relaxation of fiduciary obligations of Covid-19 vaccines.

Waiver is not enough

The acceleration of vaccine production is not solely centred around the issue of intellectual property rights. Waiver of TRIPS is an important step, but it has to be supported by transfer of technology, sharing of the know-how and also increased access to raw materials that are required for vaccine production. The WHO backed Covid-19 Technology Access Pool (C-TAP) was meant to facilitate such transfers. However, so far vaccine producing companies have refused to engage with the pool as it is a voluntary mechanism.

Also, time is the essence. Hence, even if the TRIPS relaxation were to come through, it would take time to build consensus which the world does not have and countries like India & China most certainly do not. Hence, these manufactures must tie up with local manufactures, build their capacities through on-site technology and know-how transfer through actual handholding and training and start manufacturing in that country itself without having to be concerned about breach of their intellectual property rights. This would make storage, transportation, and other logistics arrangements in the supply chain cheaper and easier to handle, thus keeping the cost of vaccines low.

Conclusion

The vaccine production and sharing schematics in mid 2021 suggested a wide inequity between the rich and the poor nations.

Whereas the richer countries were anticipated to immunize a fair share of their population by mid-2022, the poorer nations would have to wait till 2024. It should be noted that if the current vaccine inequity persisted it would lead to 2.5 million additional deaths. These deaths are avoidable, but it would call for a cohesive global effort. The rich nations would have to choose the path of cooperation over competition. They would have to support other nations in appending their institutional capacity and at the same time display leadership to circumvent regulatory hurdles. While TRIPS waiver is an important step, alternatives also have to be explored very fast as no one is safe unless everyone is safe.

1.9 Pandemic Preparedness, a primer

As India reeled under a massive second wave of the coronavirus pandemic during April-May 2021, the positive cases and deaths were rising alarmingly, forcing many states to impose limited lockdowns once again in order to curb the spread of the virus. It was required to learn and implement lessons from previous pandemics and other natural disasters.

Lessons from 1918

The Spanish Flu pandemic data shows that the second wave was the deadliest as it affected and killed more people in a short period than other waves during the entire pandemic. As data has shown so far, many countries have already experienced a major second wave and some a third one. Hence, there was no reason for us to believe that the situation would be different in India. The Covid-19 cases in India by 30 April, 2021 were at their highest level since the beginning of October 2020 and complicating matters further, some new variants of the virus were thought to be responsible for the sudden spike. Even though we were victorious in handling the first wave, we should have prepared for possible second and third waves knowing full well from history that subsequent waves are almost a certainty and have invariably been much deadlier.

Public health planning and communication should have been strengthened after the lull in cases between November 2020 - February 2021 instead of sending out mixed messages and dismantling emergency medical infrastructure deployed during the first wave and removing physical distancing restrictions too quickly. While this is certainly not the time to look in hindsight and blame governments for not doing enough or people themselves for not adhering to Covid-appropriate behaviour, we need to quickly learn and make amends—all of us!

Disaster preparedness and building redundancies

While we are dealing with the pandemic largely under the ambit of the Disaster Management Act, 2005, which established the National Disaster Management Authority (NDMA) besides the Epidemic Diseases Act, 1897 (as amended last year), all our effort after the first wave has been confined only to post-disaster response and restoration. We should have considered the other essential elements of a natural disaster management system like pre-disaster preparedness and mitigation. This was all the more important because while we confronted the first wave without any preparedness due to the once-in-a century pandemic's novelty, we could have used that experience to ramp up preparedness and mitigation measures for a possible second or third wave by building the requisite redundancies.

We should prepare a full-fledged preparedness and mitigation plan alongside a post-disaster response and recovery strategy nationally, broken down to region-wise micro-strategies framed in consultation with the states just as we currently do for a natural disaster like cyclones or floods. As a part of disaster preparedness against cyclones and floods, Odisha constructed close to a 1,000 multi-purpose cyclone shelters after the super cyclone of 1999 which, though they remain unused for most part of the year, are like hot sites ready to start functioning as and when a cyclone or flood strikes. We have seen the results of such preparedness by Odisha in the form of near zero loss of lives and property in calamities after calamities, which have been repeatedly applauded by the UN and other international agencies.

Since the 1990s with the SARS, MERS and Ebola viruses creating havoc in localised regions, the possibility of such events (pandemics) occurring had increased manifold all over the world and hence, our systems and structures like the NDMA should not look at these redundancies as a wastage of resources. If the NDMA had prepared such a plan, it would have most possibly built these redundancies to fight the sharp increase in the demand for oxygen, hospital beds and ICU facilities being faced now.

For this reason, temporary pandemic care centres at panchayat, block and district levels have to be identified and kept ready for operation at short notice; adequate supply of oxygen, oxygen beds, and equipment like ventilators and ambulances with oxygen facilities have to be ensured and deployment plans for doctors, nurses and paramedics kept ready just as Odisha had done during the first wave of the pandemic. Even though it was confronting a pandemic for the first time, the Odisha government used its previous experience in handling natural disasters to involve community and build community resilience to manage Covid, particularly in rural areas—starting from involving women SHGs for spreading awareness and distribution of ration to delegating power to district magistrates and sarpanchs. There were also separate Covid and non-Covid hospitals, and data and modelling were used to decide micro-containment strategies and plans.

Conclusion

As things stand, we should hope for the best with respect to future waves, and at the same time prepare for the worst, for what could be coming, possibly a third wave or a variant that beats the acquired or vaccine-induced antibody regime that has been discussed by experts as a distinct possibility. Governments across states should look to build medical infrastructure and redundancies in our health systems so that in future, we are not overwhelmed during such a crisis. States should be empowered to not only dip into the State Disaster Response Fund (SDRF) without awaiting approval from the Union government but also use the funding available to scale up and build acceptable levels of redundancies in medical infrastructure in the longer term.

We should continue to reinvigorate smart testing and tracing, with firm messaging on social distancing and masking. Genomic surveillance should be scaled up to track variants as early as possible to assess the efficacies of the various vaccines a priori. Supply chains for production and manufacturing medical APIs, PPE kits and medical oxygen facilities have to be augmented manifold all over the country, in every state and district.

Make no mistake, there will be subsequent waves, and India must heed the lessons from the current wave and the 1918 pandemic or else, all our efforts will be futile including vaccination.

1.10 New epidemic control and management law need of the hour

India's response to the coronavirus disease (Covid-19) pandemic has so far been effected predominantly by three different laws – the Epidemic Diseases Act, 1897 (EDA); the Disaster Management Act, 2005 (DMA); and the Indian Penal Code, 1860 (IPC). After the declaration of the pandemic as a "notified disaster", the National Executive Committee of the National Disaster Management Authority (NDMA), set up under the DMA, has been imposing the graded lockdowns and issuing periodic guidelines to states for enforcing the lockdowns. Simultaneously, both the central and state governments have fallen back on EDA to address the health aspect of this disaster. However, people violating lockdown orders were charged under sections 188, 269 and 270 of IPC.

The use of such an ad-hoc legal architecture with a multiplicity of statutes has resulted in a patchwork response against the epidemic in several areas. The archaic three-page-and-four-section EDA does not define what constitutes a "dangerous epidemic disease". It confers unbridled power to the executive to respond to the disease by the way of promulgating ordinances or regulations, but without due care to the social and reputational standing of the people affected due to the pandemic.

Similarly, DMA, passed as an immediate response to the 2004 tsunami, is largely framed for effective preparation, mitigation and managing a natural or man-made calamity, mishap or a catastrophe such as tsunamis, earthquakes and cyclones. These events are normally geographically-localised catastrophic events, disrupting normal life for a few hours or days, but unlike a public health epidemic, do not last over a long period of time. In contrast to natural disasters, physical evacuation of people from an affected area to a relatively safe zone is not an option during a pandemic due to the likelihood of the spread of the infection.

Cognisant of the lack of appropriate epidemic control and management law, in 2017, the Union ministry of health and family welfare prepared a comprehensive Public Health (Prevention, Control and Management of epidemics, bio-terrorism, and disasters) Bill to address the loopholes in the current laws including EDA. However, the Bill did not get tabled in Parliament. An Approach Paper on a new Public Health Act proposed by a 2012 task force is also gathering dust. A new and robust epidemic law must take into account the experiences and lessons learnt from the current crisis.

First, the Act should provide for an NDMA like authority or body, having representation from both the Centre and states, responsible for designing and implementing well-coordinated surveillance, identification, contact-tracing, quarantine, isolation, testing strategy and treatment. The Act must also empower the body to plan a comprehensive and reasoned lockdown strategy, taking into account disruptions to supply lines, essential and non-essential services, human migration, relief and food support and all non-health services and utilities.

Second, the Act must have provisions to allow for multi-sectoral emergency financial support and relief measures to local authorities, farmers, businesses and health care providers, and for animal care and livelihood safeguards.

Third, the Act must provide adequate autonomy to states to design and enforce responses as per their local assessments, such as preparing health facilities to respond to various challenges at the district-, block- and gram panchayat-level. For example, the Odisha Government's conferred of powers of the Collector on *sarpanches* to enforce isolation and quarantine of the migrant workers returning home from outside.

Fourth, the Act must put in a more robust disincentive scheme, which should include a combination of civil and criminal penalties for violation of authorities' orders. Currently, it provides only for criminal penalties. This should also include stringent punitive action against people abusing or mistreating frontline workers like doctors, nurses, paramedics, village-level health workers, sanitation staff and police personnel, accompanied, of course, by sufficient safeguards against overuse or misuse.

Fifth, the Act must also have provisions to protect every citizen's rights such as privacy. The balance between public health and the right to privacy must not be sacrificed at the altar of an emergency response. Any government response which involves surveillance or collection of personal data of individuals must also have adequate checks and balances to ensure proportionality and reasonableness of data collection. It must have provisions of anonymising the personal data, rigorous record-keeping, non-disclosure of personal data publicly and its deletion when the purpose of collection has been exhausted. Most importantly, there must be a clear definition of an "epidemic disease" to ensure a strict and clear boundary between the operation of an emergency statute and the resumption of ordinary laws.

Extraordinary times such as the coronavirus pandemic require extraordinary measures. But even in times of emergencies, the laws must not fall silent. Public trust is strengthened only when adequate transparency and accountability measures are put in place by governments so that the public itself is able to judge the proportionality and reasonableness of the government's actions.

1.11 Access to safe blood issue must be addressed on priority

The novel *SARS*-CoV-2 virus (Covid-19) has been causing havoc in India as well as around the globe and it has caused an unprecedented number of fatalities alongside inflicting enormous pain on the economy. Apart from the tally of direct lives lost to Covid-19, pandemics like these bring about immense inadvertent casualties; deaths due to blood shortage are one such example and it is one which can be avoided by enacting robust legislation and timely implementation of the same.

Given just how foundational blood is to healthcare, a well-equipped and organised Blood Transfusion Service (BTS) which ensures access to safe blood in a timely manner is an important component of any dependable healthcare delivery system. This holds even truer for a country like India where the trauma burden and surgical needs are large, unmet and rising.

However, data shows that the situation is somewhat grim in India, as we continue to battle a massive and consequential shortage in the provision of safe and timely blood and blood components. Our annual requirement is estimated to be at nearly 26.5 million units of blood, while the supply is just around 13.5 million units despite having an eligible donor population of more than 500 million individuals. This supply-demand disparity leaves a shortage of around 13 million units and it has had serious adverse consequences for our public health system over the years. For example, excessive bleeding after childbirth i.e. postpartum haemorrhage (PPH) accounts for nearly 30 per cent of all maternal mortality in India and regrettably, these can be well averted. Moreover, in terms of safety, in an RTI it was revealed by National AIDS Control Organisation (NACO) that 1,342 people pan-India had contracted the HIV infection due to unsafe blood transfusion in 2018-19.

What is more worrying is the fact that Covid-19 related lockdowns have seriously aggravated what was already a disturbing situation. Owing to fears of crowding, cancellation of many blood donation drives and the lack of mobility and motivation in general, the donor base has shrunk drastically and multiple media reports state how this is snowballing into a public health crisis of its own. To cite an example in October 2020, the Maharashtra State Blood Transfusion Council (SBTC) had announced that the city's blood banks had stock only for a week which highlights the severity of the issue.

In unprecedented situations like these, one can understand the benefit of social welfare initiatives like the "Jeevan Bindu" programme, which was launched by the BJD in 2015 to mark the 99th birth anniversary of former Odisha Chief Minister Shri Biju Patnaik. The initiative has now become a "People's Movement" in Odisha wherein the BJD party workers arrange blood donation camps to ensure a steady supply of safe blood. In April 2020, BJD president and Odisha Chief Minister Shri

Naveen Patnaik requested party workers to ensure availability of safe blood under the aegis of this initiative. This has helped mitigate the blood shortage situation in the state.

The Government of India had formulated a National Blood Policy (NBP) in 2002 with an aim of eliminating transfusion-transmitted infections and ensuring the provision of timely and adequate blood transfusion services to those in need. This is tied in with the larger aim of ensuring availability and accessibility of safe blood to those in need of it.

As a lawmaker, I cannot help but draw attention to the role that the lack of comprehensive blood legislation in India has had to play behind unavailability of safe and sustainable blood. The National Blood Policy on its own isn't of many effects given its provisions are recommendatory in nature and aren't backed by the force of a statute. It is interesting to note that developed societies, nearly 80 per cent of which have dedicated blood legislation enacted today account for 40 per cent of world's blood collection despite being home to just 16 per cent of the global population. India, too, should not delay the enactment of such law any further.

1.12 Lack of data to manage mental health crisis during COVID 19

The coronavirus is known to be extremely multifaceted, in the sense that it is able to attack different organs in the human body—the lungs, liver, kidneys and even the heart. However, there is another organ that the virus attacks silently, but the effects of this are most often not visible: the human mind, and that too with extremely debilitating consequences. Several reports in the past few months have highlighted a range of mental health issues stemming from the virus.

The WHO states that the lockdown(s) imposed in several countries, including India, have induced social isolation, fear, stress and anxiety in many older adults, care providers and people with underlying health conditions. Concomitant financial distress and loss of livelihoods during this period have aggravated the aforementioned issues.

Indian situation critical

A recent survey by the Indian Psychiatry Society found that the number of mental illness cases had increased by 20% since the lockdown, and that at least one in five Indians were affected. The situation is dire in India because of pre-existing neglect, ignorance and the taboo surrounding mental health as well as due to limited accessibility and availability of medical support. For instance, according to the National Mental Health Survey (2016), 83% of people suffering from mental health problems in India did not have access to treatment.

While the Mental Health Care Act of 2017 guarantees that persons with mental illness are to be treated as equal to those with any regular physical ailment, outdoor patient services still remain unavailable, resulting in people having to go to expensive private hospitals, thus increasing their out-of-pocket expenses manifold. The situation is further aggravated by the absence of insurance cover either in the public or private sector.

Amidst other mental health concerns triggered by these lockdowns, an increase in suicides has been reported. For instance, based on the latest police data, Kolkata has seen an alarming 100% increase in suicide rates since the lockdown was imposed. Diverse factors such as alcohol withdrawal, fear of contracting the virus, loss of loved ones, rising debt and economic uncertainty have played a crucial role in the alleged suicides. Student suicides in relation to competitive examinations like NEET have also been reported. Alarmingly, this has affected people and families from disenfranchised backgrounds much more acutely.

Absence of data

Concerned at the increasing suicide rates and other mental health issues, I had posed an unstarred question during the brief Monsoon Session of Parliament (252nd Session). The ministry has replied that no study was conducted by the government to assess the pandemic's impact on mental health, which is a pity if true. It must be considered that assessing the pandemic's impact on the mental well-being of the public is a necessary step in the prevention of suicides and in efforts to provide a healthy environment for the country's citizens.

Such data would have enabled a better understanding of this complex issue and resulted in the production of better health-related research and policies. In fact, the primary reason for absence of insurance products for mental health patients is the lack of data on mortality and morbidity related to this disease. Except Odisha's Biju Swasthya Kalyan Yojana, where cost of treatment of psychiatric disorders is covered with free treatment in government hospitals, most other states do not cover it. Though Ayushman Bharat covers this, insurance is not available in private hospitals. Although the government has taken several initiatives to indicate that mental health is not missing from its agenda, it cannot be denied that a thorough follow-up of the efficacy, availability, accessibility, affordability and quality is not possible unless there is accurate data. Furthermore, with nationwide variations in health and disease distribution, any mental well-being plan needs to address not only regional and state-wise differences but also a lack of awareness amongst a majority of Indians who stigmatise the disease, particularly in rural areas.

Most important is the equity aspect that needs to be kept in mind while designing and implementing any mental health policy. Therefore, to address the wide range of mental health issues, especially during this period of crisis, what we need is a tailor-made approach to the different regions and socio-cultural groups instead of a one-size-fits-all package that can only be designed if there is adequate data collected.

Conclusion

Finally, mental health issues need to be embedded in a broader public health discourse to allow for it to be treated like any other health issue as envisaged in our national health policies and programmes; only then can effective community participation take place. Any plan to manage mental health issues should also consider the parameters of age and sex. For instance, according to a recent study, 27% of women reported an increase in challenges associated with mental illness as compared to 10% of men. Medical experts warn that amidst the pandemic, a nationwide mental health crisis is imminent, which is the silent pandemic waiting to happen unless addressed immediately.

1.13 Tackling Malnutrition

India faces a huge burden of malnutrition rooted in its social, economic, and cultural asymmetries and challenges. According to the National Family Health Survey (NFHS)-4 conducted in 2014-15, for children under five years of age, 38.4 per cent were stunted (height-for-age), 21 per cent were wasted (weight-for-height), 7.5 per cent were severely wasted (weight-for-height), 35.8 per cent were underweight (weight-for-age) and 58.6 per cent were anaemic. These alarming statistics have further worsened, despite several targeted service delivery schemes and outreach programmes by the government. As per the NFHS-5 conducted in 2019, stunting has gone up in 13 states and wasting has gone up in 12 out of 22 states and UTs surveyed, respectively. This abysmal situation is further exacerbated by the emergence of COVID-19 which is expected to push many more children into malnutrition. The worsening situation of malnutrition in India demands urgent attention and resources to prevent any further backsliding on nutrition indicators. With the revival of Mission Poshan and an allocation of Rs 20,105 crore earmarked for the new national nutrition programme, the government has shown intent to tackle malnutrition.

However, to fight the chronic burden of malnutrition and the simultaneous increase in severe acute malnutrition (SAM) in a holistic manner, more concerted efforts are needed. To achieve India's "Sustainable Goal" target of reducing under-five mortality by 25 per cent by 2030, the country needs to revamp its strategy and adopt new methods of combating SAM.

Apart from the most popular method of treating children with acute malnutrition at the Bal Sewa Kendra (BSK) or Child Malnutrition Treatment Centres (MTCs), Community Management of Acute Malnutrition (CMAM) is a proven approach to manage SAM in children under five. CMAM involves timely detection and treatment of SAM children without medical complications with ready-to-use-nutrient-dense-foods at the community level itself. At a time when the pandemic has disastrously upended access to basic healthcare for far-flung communities, leveraging this opportunity will go a long way in ensuring the last-mile delivery of health care services, should there be any other disruptions in the future.

In 2015, the Odisha government piloted CMAM in tribal-dominated Kandhamal district which had the highest levels of under 5-year child mortality in the state in 2012–13. A standard CMAM approach consisted of setting-up of treatment sites closer to the community, weekly monitoring of uncomplicated SAM children, an in-patient facility to admit children with SAM and associated medical complications along with provision of Modified Energy Dense Nutritional Food (EDNRF), Modified Hot Cook Meal (HCM) and Modified Take Home Ration (THR).

The targeted programme resulted in children achieving the desired weight after treatment, thereby significantly improving the nutritional status in the district. In fact, Odisha's success in community-led and community-managed experiments in several fields including disaster management, forest management and waste management have become legendary now with only Kerala giving it some competition.

However, while Kerala has been a forbearer of such praxis since long, Odisha has been able to reach this level in just the last 20 years with the advent of the Mission Shakti Programme — a scheme to organise women into self-help groups first as a livelihood initiative. In a similar vein, Rajasthan, Gujarat, and Uttar Pradesh are some of the other states that have also shown effectiveness towards this approach.

According to the CMAM Association of India, ready-to-use-nutrient-dense-food can ensure the recovery of a SAM child in two to three months at the community level in most of the cases and reduce the need for treatment at MTCs, ultimately reducing the chances of infections and the overall cost of treatment.

Intially, India did not have a framework or a set of guidelines to address the treatment and the prevention of SAM in children. But with the release of national guidelines for POSHAN 2.0, it is essential to streamline and integrate CMAM as a routine part of the government system.

Since, CMAM has the potential to tackle severe acute malnutrition by strengthening community health systems, a collaborative effort at the community level will ensure the efficient delivery of sustainable healthcare in times to come. Additionally, while prioritising SAM, learnings from best practices of other states, will hold the key to tackle the growing burden of malnutrition.

According to a study by Lancet 2019, multiple forms of malnutrition (MOM) reduce nearly 8 per cent of a nation's economic growth. As the wealth of the nation depends not only on the skills and knowledge but health and nutrition of its people, it is high time that India caters to its eight million SAM children, if it aspires to be a $5-trillion economy by 2024-25.

1.14 Antimicrobial resistance the next big threat to mankind

The Covid-19 pandemic has taken everyone around the globe by surprise. No sooner were the first cases reported, it spread like wildfire and left behind a trail of destruction. The inherent weaknesses of the healthcare system globally lay bare. The pandemic has brought about an unprecedented number of fatalities and as of November 6, 2020 the number of deaths globally stood at 1.23 million.

However, another public health issue which has silently been gaining ground and needs the attention of stakeholders is antimicrobial resistance. To comprehend the graveness of AMR, it is crucial to appreciate the importance of antibiotics in modern medicine. These medicines are necessary to cure a whole range of ailments from simple infections to complicated surgeries as well as treatment and management of illnesses such as cancer. Antimicrobial resistance occurs when bacteria and other microbes become resistant to antibiotics due to excessive exposure and consequently, the antibiotic is unable to kill them. In such cases, the bacteria stop responding to antibiotics, and the illness/infection triggered by these bacteria becomes problematic or even impossible to treat. In fact, compare this to the death toll attributed to Covid-19, and the number of lives lost due to antimicrobial resistance (AMR) can potentially be a lot higher in the years to come. A report submitted by the Interagency Coordination Group on Antimicrobial Resistance to the UN Secretary-General in 2019 stated that over 700,000 lives are lost due to AMR each year and without targeted interventions, this number is set to reach 10 million per year by 2050, with almost a fifth of fatalities occurring in India. This was before the Covid-19 crisis was on the horizon. Now, with overuse of hand sanitisers and increased hospital admissions for Covid-19 followed with pre-emptive administration of antibiotics to about 92 per cent of the patients, the earlier quoted fatality figure almost seems like a best-case scenario.

AMR can also cause a significant setback to India achieving its stated health targets. India has set a target that by 2025 it will eliminate all case of tuberculosis. India had an estimated 130,000 drug-resistant TB cases in 2018. However, only 44 per cent or around 58,347 of the estimated multidrug-resistant cases were diagnosed. AMR is certainly going to impede the progress made through dedicated research, investment and hard work of our scientists, medical professionals, and healthcare workers and needs immediate attention of the regulators. There are several economic costs that come with AMR as well. From costlier treatment and medicines, lengthier stays in the hospital, complicated procedures, and requirement of more intensive care – all these steadily add to the catastrophe. Naturally, the impact would be felt more intensely by low and middle-income countries, furthering deepening economic inequality as well as the resource gaps.

Factors behind the rise of AMR are dynamic and evolving, but there indeed are a few key sources that can be identified. Abuse of antibiotics for treatment of illnesses and indiscriminate use in the livestock industry for increasing production are the most common reasons. But for India with its booming pharmaceutical industry which jointly with China, produces as much as 80 per cent of the global stock of antibiotics, the larger concern should be the release of untreated effluents from pharmaceutical industries. The National Action Plan on AMR released by the Central Government in 2017 does reflect a multi-sectoral One Health approach, but a crucial medium-term action point delineating the need to develop standards for antibiotic residues in industrial effluents is still missing. This remains a crucial blind spot in our fight against the challenges that AMR pose, one which policymakers need to take immediate note of.

The environment ministry had released draft standards for antibiotic residues in effluents from the pharmaceutical industry back in January 2020. Nearly nine months later, there has been no notable progress towards the finalization and notification of these standards.

This is not the time to delay regulatory action on pressing health priorities. The ball is in the government's court. Moreover, with the onset of the global pandemic and for reasons as described earlier, the clock is ticking faster than it ever has before. Bringing in the legislation to ensure effluents from antibiotic manufactured plants are treated can go a long way in helping India contain its AMR burden.

CHAPTER 2

COVID 19, CHILDREN AND HUMAN RIGHTS

2.1 NHRC's advisory on Children: A beacon of hope?

Estimating the impact of Covid-19 on children, the United Nations has observed that in some cases 'mitigation measures may inadvertently do more harm than good' and for some children, the impact will be for life. Among those hardest hit are children belonging to socio-economically backward and marginalised communities. The UNICEF has reckoned that 120 million children could fall into extreme poverty and an additional 3.9 million children could suffer from malnourishment in South Asia attributable to causes related to Covid-19. Noting these impacts, the National Human Rights Commission (NHRC) issued an 'Advisory for Protection of the Rights of Children in the context of Covid-19'in late September of 2019 which though looked comprehensive, however, falls too short of incorporating a rights-based response.

Left out children

The recommendations completely ignore the extreme vulnerabilities attached to international displacements, i.e., children of refugees, stateless persons, undocumented migrants, and asylum seekers (children of 'people of concern'). According to UNHCR 2019, 207,334 people of concern are residing in India. These individuals often lack access to mainstream social protection schemes due to tenuous legal status. As reported by UNICEF, 50 per cent migrant and refugee respondents in the age groups of 14-24 years indicated challenges in accessing healthcare. Albeit, India allows refugees to approach public health care facilities but weak governance, social stigma and discrimination inhibit such access. Besides, access is only allowed for 'registered' refugees, thereby precluding innumerable people of concern from availing healthcare.

Further, the advisory does not address the socio-economic needs of children becoming orphan due to Covid-19. Studies had estimated that the global toll of Covid-19 could reach 40 million, inevitably leaving many children without primary caregivers. Orphan-hood (arising out of pandemics such as Ebola, HIV, AIDS) has had a direct nexus with exploitation—sexual and non-sexual, emotional distress, psychosocial outcomes and child labour.

Non-Universalisation of nutritional services

Another critical issue is non-recognition of universal access to nutritional services for children outside the ICDS ecosystem. The requirement to update PDS to include children born after 2011 is a welcome move. However, according to population projections, 108 million Indians do not appear on the list of NFSA ration cards as of 2020. Updating millions of ration cards is a mammoth task, especially in an ongoing pandemic. In many states, applications for ration cards are pending in lakhs – in Jharkhand alone, 7 lakh applications are pending. More importantly, even if PDS rolls are updated, a substantial number of marginalised children will still be excluded from it, for reasons ranging from identification barriers to bureaucratic impediments. The fact that those who are not covered under PDS will be catered by community kitchens is erroneous since only five states run these kitchens.

Who's protecting children from data breach?

With widespread lockdown and social distancing norms, Covid-19 has impacted 90 per cent of the student population. More than ever, children are using the internet for learning purposes, socialisation and other activities, largely unaware that they are putting at risk their personal data. If this data is breached, it can potentially harm children in the long term. Yet, the advisory is silent on protecting children's data at the hands of ed-tech companies, video streaming platforms etc.

Data breach in case of children is not uncommon. Recently Unacademy, one of the largest ed-tech companies in India reported a data breach of 22 million users, mostly school-going children. Taking cognizance on a plea stating that there isn't any law governing age eligibility for accessing social media in India, the Supreme Court in 2020 issued notice to the central government seeking its response on the matter. However, the situation clamours a detailed protocol.

Lack of economic and social rehabilitation measures

Apart from food and health, distressed children require economic and social support. The biggest limitation of the government advisory was that it did not provide any additional economic or social rehabilitation support to marginalised children. Such measures include social security benefits like vocational training, skill development, cash assistance, setting up shelters etc. Law enforcement alone will not curtail child marriages, child labour or trafficking. We must keep in mind that in a pandemic setting, children are driven to these precarious conditions owing to financial challenges faced by their families. In Sierra Leone during Ebola, 43% of children were engaged in child labour while girls turned to transactional sex to support their families.

Many countries are providing aid to children. The USA, for instance, has pledged $45 million specifically for prevention of family violence and responsive services for children. Such measures can be enacted in India too, for which the funds can be mobilised from various cess funds lying unutilised such as Construction Workers Cess Fund and District Mineral Funds.

Conclusion

Covid-19 is an unprecedented crisis and requires unprecedented solutions. The advisory issued by NHRC in 2021 was a beacon of hope, but unless the loopholes are fixed, the possibility of protecting India's children is still a distant dream.

2.2 The perils of Child marriage

The Covid-19 pandemic has made girls all over the world even more vulnerable to the menace of child marriage. A profoundly regressive practice, child marriage is an unquestionable violation of human rights, the result of several intricately intertwined factors, among which are patriarchy, poverty and the lack of education. A report by the United Nations Population Fund states that the pandemic is projected to result in 13 million additional child marriages which might otherwise have been prevented. It has also been suggested by the international children's charity, World Vision, that the pandemic has the potential to put an extra four million girls at risk of early marriage.

One of the major reasons for this spike is poverty, induced and escalated by Covid-19. To survive in this pandemic, economically disenfranchised parents often resort to child marriage to escape the financial burden of caring for a girl child. The Odisha State Commission for Protection of Child Rights has corroborated the growing trend of child marriages as a result of the pandemic. Since April 2020, more than 180 attempted child marriages have been reported in Odisha according to various district child welfare officers. Another incentive for poverty-stricken families is that younger brides often require smaller dowries or command higher bride prices. The closure of schools during this national health crisis has also left young girls extremely vulnerable to forced marriage. Several media reports have corroborated these facts.

Concerned with such reports, I had raised an unstarred question during the 252nd brief Monsoon Session of Parliament. Surprisingly, the ministry's response was arbitrary and inexplicable, claiming that as per the information received from the National Crime Records Bureau, there was no data to indicate a rising number of child marriages in India. Despite sufficient circumstantial evidence to suggest an increase, the response to the question ostensibly means that neither the government has maintained a database on child marriages during the lockdown nor has it conducted any in-depth survey. The NCRB either did not collect such data, or such acts do not get reported as crimes. Thus, sadly, there is not even an acknowledgment of this simmering crisis. This is where the problem lies.

The lack of a data-driven, evidence-based approach seriously jeopardizes troubleshooting and beneficiary mapping. It prevents the government from addressing the phenomenon. Further, the paucity of data limits the government's understanding of how to tackle the crisis. Thus, it is imperative for the government to conduct studies and surveys and collect in-depth data to understand the prevailing ground realities concerning child marriages in India during the pandemic.

Although the government's consideration to raise the minimum age of marriage for girls from 18 to 21 has been lauded as a progressive move, this alone would not be enough to tackle the menace of child marriage. It might even be counterproductive; there might be a further persecution of girls by their families until the age of 21. Regressive social practices against women are deep-seated in patriarchal society. From the time they are born, girls must have access to education, career opportunities, right to choices regarding marriage and so on. Gender sensitisation and awareness programmes should also be made mandatory in schools.

In order to abolish child marriages, the government needs to take cues from UNICEF which centres its work on five key interventions: adolescents as agents of change, social mobilisation among parents and within communities, investments in education for children both in and out of school, access to social protection programmes and linkages with skills and employment opportunities. These interventions are in tandem with India's commitment to eliminating child marriage by 2030 as part of the sustainable development goals.

First, the government needs to acknowledge that child marriages perpetuate a vicious cycle of poverty, weakens the development of a skilled workforce, reinforces gender inequality and has a detrimental impact on the health of society and the economy. India has made notable progress in reducing child marriage: the UNICEF data from March 2018 states that 25 million child marriages have been prevented in the last decade. However, the same data also highlights that considerably more work is needed in the aftermath of the pandemic. Else, by 2030 more than 120 million girls will be forcefully married before their 18th birthday. This is a grim reminder that we have to move fast and decisively.

2.3 Need for a strong anti-trafficking law

Since early 2020, humanity has been under siege. While globally several countries have had their share of recoveries and relapses, the Covid-19 pandemic, particularly the second wave, has put India under considerable strain. The pandemic exposed and exacerbated the systemic and deeply entrenched socio-economic inequities in Indian society, thus increasing manifold the consequential vulnerability and marginality. The disruption in economic activities across sectors, massive rise in unemployment and sources of livelihood have put a sizable population of India under desperate circumstances.

A study by Azim Premji University estimates that nearly 230 million Indians have fallen below the poverty line since the pandemic. The vulnerable populace reeling under such desperation makes the perfect recipe for exploitation. One such form of exploitation that we need to be vigilant about is human trafficking. As many as 27 lakh distress calls were made to the Ministry of Women and Child Development between March and August 2020. Between April 2020 and June 2021, over 9,000 children were rescued from traffickers.

Human trafficking places vulnerable people in highly exploitative situations, stripping victims of their freedom and choice. Besides, it is a highly lucrative organised crime that amounts to a billion-dollar industry. India lacks an over-arching law on human trafficking although there are a multitude of laws that deal with different forms of trafficking. In such a context, the Trafficking in Persons (Prevention, Care and Rehabilitation) Bill 2021 is both necessary and pertinent. The current Bill represents a significant departure from the Trafficking in Persons 2018 Bill, which failed to take into consideration the plight of trafficked victims. The 2018 Bill was criticised and failed to pass muster in Parliament.

In contrast, the new Bill is victim-centric and prioritises the dignity, care and rehabilitation of trafficked victims. There are various welcome additions and changes to this Bill when compared with the Trafficking of Persons Bill, 2018. These include:

a) definitions of 'exploitation', 'sexual exploitation', 'rehabilitation';
b) defined responsibilities of the national, state and district anti-human trafficking committees;
c) measures to ensure dignity, care, rehabilitation and reintegration of victims;
d) provision of interim relief and rehabilitation not contingent on prosecution;
e) free legal aid and support to victims to seek compensation;
f) placing the onus of filing the FIR on the investigating officer and;
g) more stringent punishment to offenders.

This will ensure clarity for investigating agencies in prosecution and for courts to interpret the law.

While the Bill defines rehabilitation and places emphasis on ensuring the same for survivors, it does not specify a dedicated rehabilitation fund. A dedicated fund must be maintained for relief, rehabilitation, victim compensation, and funds for inter and intra-state investigations. Without these allocated funds, the institutions will not be able to carry out their responsibilities in a timely and efficient manner.

Besides, rehabilitation is limited to shelter homes with no provision for reintegration and community-based rehabilitation. Community-based rehabilitation, a model that provides health services, legal aid, access to welfare schemes and income opportunities, is crucial for ensuring the reintegration of victims back into their community and family. The risk of re-trafficking is high unless the victims are provided economic support. The inclusion of job training and skill development in the rehabilitation process will empower victims to be financially independent and provide them with freedom and choice. This is particularly imperative in the pandemic and post-pandemic context.

In addition, the Bill must provide greater agency to survivors to choose the duration of stay at shelter homes. This is necessary to provide them with the freedom to leave the institution if there is any exploitation and abuse, which are commonly reported. Equally important is to have checks and balances in place to ensure that shelter homes are safe places for survivors.

Anti Human Trafficking Units (AHTUs) are a central institution in the present anti-human trafficking ecosystem. They have been responsible for the timely investigation of trafficking cases and for ensuring the care and dignity of victims. However, the Bill does not mention AHTUs except once, thus failing to both clarify their role as well as to strengthen their functioning. Though various states have set up AHTUs, we do not have anything uniform throughout the country that will make it mandatory that AHTUs investigate human trafficking cases. Therefore, a law that would set out the procedures and clarify what will be taken up by which body, is essential. Assigning this responsibility and accountability to one body that is responsible solely for human trafficking will ensure speedy investigations and aid to survivors.

The Government of Odisha has been working relentlessly to address the issue through various measures including allocating Rs 9 crore for the strengthening of AHTUs, working toward efficient inter-departmental coordination, creating various support systems for women and girls to help combat vulnerabilities, setting up help lines among others. This model of strengthening AHTUs has been successful in Odisha and should be extended to other states as well through this law.

2.4 Custodial deaths in India

The rule of law is the foundation of a just and democratic society. It requires a fair and effective criminal justice system in which the police have a central role to play. The police is the most recognisable face of the State. The sheer range of the duties and tasks assigned to them require both, adequate and modern infrastructure, as well as sensitive and well-trained personnel. It is essential to build capacities of our police persons for not only upholding the law but also in constitutional conduct and compassionate handling of crises involving all sections of citizens. India aspires to be, and rightly so, an economic superpower with prosperity for all its citizens. But it is also true that India's future as a democracy and an economic powerhouse cannot be secured by an obsolete criminal justice system where the police works for the rulers of the day and not for the real masters, the people of the country. The police in a just and democratic setup, has to be made responsive to the prevailing and emerging needs of this new India.

The death of Mr. Jayaraj and his son Mr. Fenix in June 2020 is a tragic reminder of the gross abuse of power and the brutality of custodial torture. Violation of human rights has become a common occurrence in our country today. We have been seeing repeated media reports over the last few years of police crossing the line and taking the law into their own hands-breaking the bones of people accused of theft, extrajudicial encounters, targeting journalists and students who dissent against the government's policies and more recently during the COVID19 pandemic, harassment of the public under the pretext of enforcing lockdowns. Currently, the act governing the Indian Police, the 'Indian Police Act of 1861,' which is Victorian-era legislation under which disciplining the police was not a priority. The 'Status of Policing in India Report – 2019' found that 2 out of 5 police personnel surveyed in Bihar, and 1 out of 5, in six other States, had never received Human Rights training. Without proper training, most police personnel believe in violence towards criminals, whether accused or convicted. As per a report released by a consortium of NGOs against custodial torture, 1,731 people have died in custody in India during 2019. This works out to around five custodial deaths a day.

Practices around the world

The police force is commonly identified as one of the most corrupt governmental institutions. The cases of Hong Kong, Norway, Germany and Spain highlight how determined police administrations, continuous political commitment, and an anti-corruption approach with wide alliances between the public, private and civil society sectors, can make a huge difference in anti-corruption reform efforts. Police in Finland and Norway, for example, require that officers seek permission before shooting anyone, where possible. In Spain, police must provide verbal cautions and warning shots before resorting to deadly force. Even in circumstances where weapons aren't used, police officers in Europe tend to be more restricted in what they can do. Key to that challenge is revamping the training for prospective officers. In Germany, for example, police recruits are required to spend two and a half to four years in basic training to become an officer, with the option to pursue the equivalent of a bachelor's or master's degree in policing. In the case of Hong Kong, organisational reforms to the Police Force along with legal and regulatory instruments are put in place to ensure disciplinary measures on officers guilty of offences.

International Convention against torture

Every Custodial death in India is a reminder as to why India must ratify the Convention against torture. The UN Convention against torture and other cruel, inhuman or degrading treatment or punishment was adopted as a resolution on 10th December 1984 and came into force on 26th June 1987. It is an international human rights treaty aimed to prevent torture and other acts of cruel, inhuman or degrading treatment around the world. India stands behind 161 nations, including Pakistan, as it is yet to ratify the 30-year-old United Nations' Convention against Torture. India is part of a unique list of nine countries along with Sudan, Brunei, Bahamas, Sao Tome and Principe, Angola, Comoros, Gambia and Palau. These countries have the inglorious distinction of not having ratified the UN Convention Against torture (CAT).

Conclusion

A multi-pronged approach toward police anti-corruption is the need of the hour. Firstly, it is imperative to create an institutional structure that discourages rent-seeking behaviour by the police. Secondly, the development of a values-based framework within the police force should be facilitated for the creation of a corruption-free organisational setup. In particular, emphasis should be placed on professionalism, integrity and honesty so as to establish a service-oriented police culture. Thirdly, the high degree of fairness and predictability in determining the pay and benefits of police force personnel should be considered as a factor to discourage police corruption. Lastly, an adequate and effective mechanism should be put in place to fight any excesses of police authority. The police force has turned into an unrestrained beast because of the lack of reforms, lack of accountability and the habit of using force, fear and intimidation. We need stringent reforms and strict monitoring agencies if we are to reign in the alarming cases of atrocities by men in uniform. These incidents will need to be strictly punished if we want to reinstate the public's faith in the police and the law. The people must not fear the police more than lawlessness itself. This is the kind of bottom-up police reform that is urgently required. We do not live in some feudal monarchy or a police state. This is a democracy.

2.5 Decriminalizing offences – Is it the right approach?

The Union finance ministry had in June 2020 proposed decriminalisation in as many as 36 sections across 19 laws, including the Negotiable Instruments Act, SARFAESI Act, LIC Act, PFRDA Act, RBI Act, Banking Regulation Act, and Chit Funds Act, etc. The ministry saw this as an attempt to improve ease of doing business, and unclog the court system and prisons. It was also stated to be a significant step towards fulfilling the government of India's objective of 'sabka saath, sabka vikas, sabka vishwaas'.

One of the major laws that have caught the public eye in all this is the decriminalisation of section 138 of the Negotiable Instruments (NI) Act 1881, which deals with dishonour of cheques. Cheques getting returned because of inadequacy of funds in a bank account, and other such causes, is an offence under the NI Act. The law provides for two-year imprisonment and a fine equivalent to twice the amount involved. The objective of this was to promote the efficiency of banking operations and to ensure credibility and trust (vishwaas) in transacting business through cheques, as held in Modi Cements Ltd. Vs. Kuchil Kumar Nandi [(1998) 3 SCC 249]. This section incorporates a strict liability on the issuer of the instrument in so far as cheque, a negotiable instrument, is concerned. Generally, in criminal law, 'mens rea' is an essential component of a crime, but dishonour of cheque is a criminal offence where there is no need of proving this. Strict liability in this section has proven to be an effective measure to ensure the discharge of debts in transactions, and has, in fact, built an environment of trust in commercial transactions, particularly in the B2C and C2C segments.

The government's move to decriminalise it comes as a major blow to banks, creditors and other suppliers as it will substantially affect the recovery of their dues. It would also harm the credit culture in the country which had somewhat improved due to the criminal element in the NI Act. The deterrence that Sec 138 imposed on the cheque-writer would also be compromised as issuing of false cheques would no longer attract criminal liability, and after the proposed amendment comes into action, civil courts would be clogged with cheque bounce cases which would take years to resolve as it happened earlier. The corresponding provisions in developed countries like US, UK, Singapore, etc, is dealt with criminal charges of 'deposit account fraud' or 'forgery', though without strict liability jurisprudence.

The government is also sought to decriminalise contravention of Section 29 of the Sarfaesi Act. This provides for imprisonment and penalty, and gives banks the powers to recover dues from a defaulting borrower by selling properties offered as collateral. Legislations abroad similar to the Sarfaesi law also have similar provisions. However, converting this into a civil offence would force creditors to wait longer to recover their legitimate dues, and thereby put banks under increasing pressure of NPAs, something that the government is currently trying to tackle.

Changes were proposed to Insurance Act, Pension Fund Regulatory & Development Authority Act (PFRDA), RBI Act,

Payment and Settlement Systems Act, NABARD Act, Banning of Unregulated Deposit Schemes Act, Chit Funds Act, among others. Some of these offences included holding a violent demonstration that prevents normal functioning of a bank or undermines the confidence of depositors, which, according to section 36 AD of Banking Regulation Act, attracts a jail term of six months and Rs 1,000-penalty. The law-makers instated criminal overtones to the various sections of these legislations so as to deter individuals from committing such offences, which may not seem alarming, but could affect adversely the environment of trust (vishwaas).

While the proposal to decriminalise minor offences is touted to provide relief to foreign investors for whom criminal liability for economic offences is a big concern, it will have a negative impact on creditors who will have to wait longer to recover their legitimate dues. Pendency of cases has always haunted India's judicial system, be it civil or criminal matters. However, the pendency in case of civil matters is worse than that of criminal cases. Hence, this move would only add to woes of the civil courts, merely shifting the burden from criminal to civil courts. Besides, the context and the business environment that necessitated the change from civil to criminal liability have not changed much. In some legislations like the Banning of Unregulated Deposit Schemes Act and the Chit Funds Act, the impact of such change remains unassessed because the changes were brought in 2019 and not a lot of time has lapsed to assess the benefits. Until courts are made more efficient, the purpose of decriminalising offences will be defeated, and will hurt the banking system and the very business environment that the government seeks to improve by bringing in such dilution.

CHAPTER 3

ODISHA'S LESSONS IN COVID GOVERNANCE AND INCLUSIVE GROWTH MODEL

3.1 Odisha's emergence as a leader in Covid Management

The first state-wide information, education and communication (IEC) outreach about the coronavirus in Odisha was conducted on March 8, 2020, the same day when the first international passenger was screened in the state. Two days later, the state government declared COVID-19 to be a 'disaster'. The state also empowered public officials to combat the spread under the Disaster Management Act 2005 and imposed the Epidemic Disease Act 1897 where necessary.

The next day, masks, gloves and sanitisers were qualified as essential commodities and a database of all persons arriving in Odisha from other states was activated. The state also declared an incentive of Rs 15,000 for anyone who had returned to Odisha and self-imposed a 14-day home quarantine.

At this point, when the chief minister was addressing the state to prepare for a pandemic which could last for six months, the number of cases in the state stood at zero and the first case was diagnosed only on March 16, 2020.

Odisha barely features on the list of well performing public health systems in the country. In NITI Aayog's Health Index 2019, Odisha did not even feature in the top ten among large states. Kerala, unsurprisingly, topped the index and was lauded for its response to COVID-19, with reports that the curve already flattened in the state. However, on April 25, 2020 when India's COVID-19 case count stood at about 26,283, Odisha was posting numbers in double digits at 94 cases and on April 30, 2020 it was 33,067 and 142 positive cases, respectively. It could be argued that COVID-19 never picked up in the state which is not exactly known for an effective health system.

Since the beginning, the state's response to the pandemic has seen increased testing, effective resource allocation, swift private sector partnerships, infrastructure set-up, capacity building of human resources in health care, and incentives for citizens to test. This may have directly resulted in a low case confirmation ratio, low case fatality rate, and a high recovery and discharge ratio. Odisha's COVID-19 management strategy could offer insights into effective pandemic management.

Resource mobilisation and decentralised outreach

The chief minister's alert to prepare for a six-month pandemic was followed by advanced disbursement of welfare resources to the entitled beneficiaries. About 48 lakh pensioners were paid for the next four months and 82 lakh ration card holders received ration stocks for three months. Students also received pre-matriculation scholarships for the following three months.

Panchayats emerged as central to the state's communication and response strategy. Rs 5 lakh were disbursed to each panchayat to set up temporary medical camps and to equip them for any unforeseen need for basic amenities. By April 14, 2020, 7276 temporary medical camps with a total of 1,62,659 beds had been set up across 6798 gram panchayats in the state with a nodal representative appointed at each. Awareness meetings were being conducted with each panchayat and zila parishad as early as March 19, 2020 with extensive information campaigns on COVID-19, its prevention and case reporting. Swachchta Sathis were made responsible for awareness programmes at the zila parishad level. In another push for a decentralised response, the state directed the inclusion of required manpower for different activities to counter COVID-19, procurement of materials for temporary health camps, provision for infrastructure including toilets, hiring of ambulances and other vehicles for transportation of patients, provision of food, and drinking water to the Local Area Development (LAD) funds of the state's MLAs.

Capacity building and response infrastructure

The state's response to educate the healthcare personnel was to use online training programmes. To provide informed healthcare in the state, about 500 faculty members and staff of medical institutions, 1,600 medical officers of AYUSH, and about 900 residents and faculty members of dental colleges were trained in basic management through video-conferencing apps. Among frontline health workers, about 5,542 nursing students, 1.17 lakh ASHAs and auxiliary nurse midwives were trained online.

The state also designated 'coronavirus hospitals' across Odisha, with 31 such hospitals as on April 24, 2020 the latest of which was a 200-bed facility in Sambalpur. The state has been quick to partner with existing non-government hospitals, including those in the private sector by signing agreements specific to their roles and contribution to the state's response. Involvement of medical colleges and private hospitals meant an addition of at least 1,500 hospital beds.

Migrants' database and cash incentives

Odisha had prepared a database of returning migrants before the chief minister's alert and the first case in the state. On the day of the national lockdown, the state government knew 78,233 persons had returned to Odisha from other states, with district and panchayat specific tally. The data was shared with gram panchayats and the panchayat samitis and district administration was intimated about those arrivals. Through IEC, the state had already prepared panchayat members on encouraging returning migrants to self-isolate or quarantine. However, to incentivise self-isolation of returning migrants, the state had announced a cash incentive of Rs 15,000 to all those who had completed home quarantine according to the standard operating procedures issued by the state. To motivate the healthcare staff, the chief minister then announced early disbursement of salaries for all healthcare personnel in the state.

COVID-19 spread in Odisha

The total number of cases in Odisha on April 30, 2020 – when total cases in India were at 33,067 – stood at just 142, of which 55 had recovered. On only four days thus far, the state had registered cases in the double digits (Till 5 May, 2020). Importantly, the recovery ratio in the state stood at 38% compared to 25% nationally. During the said time, the state saw only one death keeping the fatality rate at 0.7% compared to 3.2% nationally and about 7% globally.

Early and comprehensive response seems to be paying off

The low number of cases in Odisha didn't appear to be due to a low number of tests. Odisha had by then conducted about 723 tests per million people compared to the national average of about 519. The case confirmation ratio – the percentage of cases that are positive out of total tested – was 0.4% for Odisha against the national case confirmation ratio of 3.5%.

The Indian Council of Medical Research had used the sample test multiple – the number of tests required to identify each new patient – as an indicator of spread. India was detecting one new case after about 24 tests during that time, while in Odisha, a new case was being identified after 223 samples, as on April 30, 2020.

Flattening the curve

Most states in India had increased the number of tests per day since the lockdown began, but a high number of tests per million and a high number of tests required to identify a positive case indicated that COVID-19 may not have spread in the state of Odisha as much as in some others. The number of cases in Odisha never rose exponentially and the growth was linear. Odisha's timely on-ground preparedness and decentralised information campaigns showed an impact. Overall, Odisha rightly strategized to manage the pandemic.

3.2 Boosting isolation ward capacity in COVID 19

On March 14, 2020 the Ministry of Home Affairs notified Covid-19 as a 'disaster', invoking the Disaster Management Act, 2005. In mounting an effective response at its level, the

Odisha Government drew from its experience, strategy and infrastructure in contending with cyclonic events in recent years and declared the outbreak a disaster on March 12, before a single case was detected within the State. The State published the Covid-19 Regulations, 2020, alongside an initial fund of Rs 200 crore to tackle the spread of the virus.

As a whole, the nation did well to commence screening of international arrivals from affected countries, or those presenting symptoms of the disease. However, Odisha could not wait for guidance from the Central Government, which itself was grappling with the spread of the virus nationally. Understanding the need for an effective strategy, Chief Minister Naveen Patnaik constituted a Group of Ministers and a Committee of Secretaries to monitor the implementation of measures. As Odisha has gradually learnt, disaster mitigation requires an advanced and comprehensive approach. The CAG (Report No. 5 of 2013) had acknowledged that Odisha had instituted a number of measures to strengthen its institutional framework post the 1999 Super Cyclone.

The crux of this strategy has been building community preparedness and involvement, thereby making people resilient to disasters of such magnitude. A vital component of this was the construction of 316 Multi-Purpose Cyclone Shelters in 6 of its coastal districts. This preparedness was put to the test when cyclone Fani made landfall in 2019. As many as 1.5 million people were shifted to 4,000 shelters within 24 hours in what would have been one of the biggest evacuations in history. Earlier, the Odisha Government's handling of cyclone Phailin was appreciated internationally for following a 'zero casualty approach' for the first time in the country.

Odisha's experience has been transposed to the coronavirus disaster as well. In terms of preparedness, MLAs were sensitised to spread the message to their constituents. Certain widespread practices also needed change. The State took this opportunity to campaign against spitting of 'paan', seen as a major health hazard. Persons have also been arrested for spreading misinformation. Further, `21 crore was sanctioned for 114 Urban Local Bodies to take preventive measures. Isolation for coronavirus is crucial in the same manner as evacuation is for cyclones. To leverage existing infrastructure, `5 lakh was released to each Panchayat to convert Panchayat buildings into isolation wards, for which ASHA and Anganwadi workers have been trained on disinfections and precautions.

Isolation wards had also been opened in CHCs and district hospitals. The government had also identified 7,276 temporary medical camps, each with a designated nodal officer, in all 6,798 Gram Panchayats for any contingencies that may arise. For mitigation, the State of Odisha initiated 'social distancing' a week prior to the Prime Minister's announcement in 2020 and closed educational institutions, gyms and cinema halls. The Health and Family Welfare Department, Collectors and Municipal Commissioners were authorised to make emergency procurement of necessary drugs and equipment. Seventy per cent of about 3,200 foreign returnees were identified as returning to six districts. These high-risk areas were locked down first. The pandemic had exposed weaknesses in the nation's preparedness against infectious diseases. The historically neglected healthcare sector came in focus. According to the World Health Organization (WHO), the country's domestic government health expenditure was estimated by at 1 per cent of its GDP in 2015, whereas the global average was 3.5 per cent.

The ancient Epidemic Diseases Act of 1897 had major limitations and was in need of an overhaul. Additional deficiencies were discovered by the CAG (Report No. 25 of 2017), which found some health centres and district hospitals functioning in unhygienic environments, inaccessible to the public, or located beyond three kilometres from the remotest village. The shortfall in staff nurses was 64 per cent, while shortfall in paramedical staff was 34 per cent against IPHS standards. These were the frontline health workers in the fight against the pandemic. Realising this shortfall, the Odisha Government had issued guidelines with clear instructions for community monitoring of quarantined homes.

Presently, disease surveillance must be prioritised. The Odisha Chief Minister's suggestions on scaling up testing facilities and inclusion of private sector had been heeded as ICMR issued guidelines for testing by private laboratories. The supply of adequate protective medical gear to doctors, nurses and first-responders also could not be compromised. These were made available at the district level.

The Odisha Government drew from its experience, strategy and infrastructure in contending with cyclonic events in recent years and declared the outbreak a disaster on March 12, 2020 even before a single case was detected within the State.

3.3 'Lockdown Success' in Odisha attributable to Effective Food Distribution

The Union Health Ministry applauded Odisha's success in limiting the spread of the virus to such a level that it took the State more than 30 days to double the number of positive detections compared to 10 days nationally, the natural corollary was that the lockdown had 'worked'.

While such a general conclusion was obvious, what was missed out was whether the people would have honoured the lockdown's principle of social distancing if food distribution amongst the population with no access to food under these circumstances was not managed efficiently?

How Odisha's Dept of Food Supply Managed to Feed Over 80% of the State

While every state was strategizing about how to manage a disaster like the COVID-19 outbreak, Odisha had its plan in place for managing the crisis at least 10 days ahead of the nationally-declared lockdown in March 2020.

At least two weeks before the first lockdown was declared by the Centre (midnight of 24 March), Odisha had started putting its resources together to ensure advanced distribution of Public Distribution System (PDS) food grains for three months, and disbursement of Rs 1000 cash to all eligible families. CM Naveen Patnaik however, ordered inclusion of more left out eligible beneficiaries under the Food Security Act, while announcing that no one should go hungry in the state.

As of 24 April, 2020 more than 4 lakh MT had already been distributed within a short period of about 30 days. The 200-odd state owned godown facilities for storing grains were operational with a total staff of 100-plus supervisors, 16,000-plus workers, and almost a thousand vehicles making contactless doorstep deliveries of PDS stocks – all while strictly maintaining social distancing norms.

Odisha Govt Has Shared Food Grains with Other States Too

In a press conference, the secretary of the department clarified that the distribution of the goods began as early as 24 March, 2020 through 12,356 Fair Price Shops in 4004 Gram Panchayats, 5922 private shops, 2034 SHGs networks and 69 Maitree shops. When public movement was curtailed to hard comply the lockdown as a medical emergency imperative, the state department arranged for home deliveries of groceries, and even cooked food for the elderly in most of the 7000-odd gram panchayats.

The government was made sure of LPG supply and availability of fuel in the market at local distribution centres.

Besides catering to the needs of the people of Odisha, the state government had sent more than 1.5 lakh MT rice to others like Jharkhand, Bihar and Tamil Nadu, a far cry from the days when Odisha had to beg the Centre for its quota of rice to feed into its own PDS system.

19 Lakh Families in Odisha Covered by Rs 185 Crore Cash Transfer

The advanced and pro-active planning of the state can be gauged from the fact that the chief minister assured food availability for the whole quarter from April to June 2020 under the NFSA (National Food Security Act), covering 66 percent of households who are eligible to receive food grains under this Act.

Under the Food Security Cover, about 19 lakh families had also been distributed Rs 185 crore in cash transfers at the rate of Rs 1000 per ration card, including 36,000 eligible new beneficiaries through active inclusion.

Besides, around twenty-four thousand 'guest workers' from other states had been given accommodation and food by the government in 336 camps.

Odisha had stood out as an example of how it ensured food security for one and all, so as to mitigate the hardships that the poor, the vulnerable and the migrants would have faced because of the prolonged lockdown. In fact, the success of the lockdown could be significantly attributed to this ability of the state government to mitigate rural food distress.

3.4 Odisha's Covid fight via Women self-help groups

Odisha did a better job than many other states in successfully handling the Covid-19 crisis because it deployed some of the key strategies that were previously put in place during cyclones and floods, which ravished the state. Some of these included marshalling the women self-help groups — SHGs — and getting the food and relief distribution models right.

The United Nations (UN) applauded Odisha for its handling of the Phailin by practising, for the first time by any state in India, a 'zero casualty' approach and achieving the same. Community participation along with swift and firm administrative actions became the hallmark of this achievement.

Massive reach of SHGs

Odisha CM Naveen Patnaik called upon the state's gigantic and ever reliable network of two lakh plus women-only self-help groups —comprising about 70 lakh women spread across all the districts, villages and gram panchayats (GPs) of the state — to help. When the first set of health advisories pertaining to symptoms, treatments, and measures to reduce the spread of coronavirus, by maintaining regular hand hygiene and social distancing were announced in March 2020, it is this network that was able to deliver these advisories by personally reaching out to every household in more than 60,000 villages in about 8,000 gram panchayats within just 3 days.

There was at least one member of each SHG going and explaining everything in person to the members of a household, besides handing out a leaflet. This brought in the kind of seriousness that was required to prevent the spread of the disease. Such a reach had never been experienced before because this massive women force had never been used earlier for administration and governance.

What surprised everyone was the promptness, efficiency and effectiveness with which this information, education and communication (IEC) activity was carried out. It is precisely for this reason that the pandemic was largely concentrated in the towns of Odisha, and did not see severe community transmission.

Similarly, when CM Naveen Patnaik appealed to everyone to take an oath to stay indoors under the Mo Jiban (My Life) programme, it was these 70 lakh women who led from the front and sent thousands and lakhs of videos showing their solidarity with the CM.

Thus, the community got involved in this preventive measure in a very unique way, not experimented earlier in the Odisha administration.

Odisha's 'home police'

When Naveen Patnaik announced that no person shall go

hungry during the lockdown, it was again this SHG network that volunteered to set up ration shops in collaboration with the local governments in every gram panchayat and village, and more importantly, even delivered the ration to homes in a few districts in mobile vans. They also home delivered more than five lakh cooked food packets in 5,247 gram panchayats to the destitute, beggars, homeless and vulnerable who couldn't even cook food. It was highly unlikely that any other official or non-official network could have achieved this coverage in such a short time.

Besides, this network produced as many as 18 lakh masks and distributed them around the state, a large chunk of it for free to the frontline Covid warriors like nurses, safai karmacharis and police personnel. A group of SHGs also contributed to the CM relief fund from their own earnings.

The women SHGs had much more daunting task in store for them. During a press conference, Sujata Karthikeyan, secretary of the Mission Shakti department that oversees women SHGs in the state, appealed to them that "About 70 lakh women SHG members, who represent their family, should also do policing in homes just as cops in uniform do."

Women leading the fight

Karthikeyan was not the only woman who is in the team of senior bureaucrats that is dealing with the crisis in Odisha. The implementation of the National Health Mission in Odisha is overseen by a woman; the state level medical corporation, which is responsible for making timely procurement is headed by a woman; and lastly, the department of women and child welfare has a woman as its chief.

The case of Odisha SHG network and its management by woman officers at the helm is a live example of a community working in tandem with the government in spreading awareness, implementing the lockdown and managing its immediate human and societal impacts. This, when highly developed countries like USA, UK, France and Italy, with their most advanced health care systems and much less population density, could not effectively stop the community spread of the disease.

These women SHGs have managed to build a robust community based on resilience and surveillance mechanism in such a short time, which would otherwise have been very difficult to achieve by any other means. The efficacy of this network was again tested when the migrant labourers returned to their villages where the Odisha government had made registration, self- isolation, quarantine and testing mandatory before they can enter their villages. These vigilant troops of women have proven to be the silent warriors in Odisha's successful tackling of the dreaded pandemic so far.

3.5 Combating malnutrition: How Odisha managed this during a pandemic?

India is home to half of the wasted children (those with a low weight for their height) globally, according to the recent Global Nutrition Report 2020. Moreover, more than a third (37.9 percent) of our children under the age of five years are stunted, and over a fifth (20.8 percent) are wasted, the report further highlights.

Malnutrition programmes in India have come under increased strain due to the COVID-19 pandemic. There are reports that the stringent national lockdown to curb the spread of COVID-19 adversely affected programmes that aim to curb malnutrition like the delivery of food under the mid-day meal scheme and the functioning of the Anganwadi centres under ICDS. As many as 115 million children depend on the mid-day meal for their daily dietary requirements.

However, the Government of Odisha under the leadership of Chief Minister Naveen Patnaik used this very otherwise well-oiled woman-led machinery to combat the challenge posed due to the pandemic.

Initiatives under the Odisha government

According to National Family Health Survey (NFHS)-4, Odisha has witnessed a steep decline in malnutrition in children under five and has been declared as a champion state. This has been made possible through a plethora of well-conceived woman- and child-centric welfare schemes and an extremely committed implementation mechanism.

In early 2020, Odisha allocated Rs 5,543 crore to introduce a one-of-a-kind nutrition budget (the first in the country) to front this decade's long fight led by Anganwadi centres, schools and health institutions. With existing policies like PDS and ICDS, the state tried to improve functionality and effectiveness of departments of Food Supply and Consumer Welfare, School and Mass Education, SC and ST Development, Health and Family Welfare, Housing and Urban Development, Panchayati Raj and Drinking Water, Agriculture and Farmers Empowerment, and Fisheries and Animal Resource Development and brought synergy within them. The budget allocation had two components — 'nutrition-specific' and 'nutrition-sensitive', to target micro-level impact along with improving overall nutritious food availability.

Odisha had also created a separate department called Mission Shakti under the Women and Child Development Ministry to intensify the focus of SHG livelihood initiatives including tackling malnutrition at the household level. Allocation of the 'nutrition budget' had also laid the foundation for Odisha Millets Mission (OMM) led by SHG women across the state, educating the masses on nutritious cooking and diet with a mobile kitchen model.

Odisha's 4 Cs approach

Call for action: Odisha's chief minister Naveen Patnaik alerted the administration as well his party, the Biju Janata Dal, with a call for action as early as the first week of March, 2020. While declaring a statewide lockdown, he urged people to strictly follow social distancing but deployed statewide resources to ensure ample food supply for everyone for the next quarter.

Collective action: The state departments collectively mobilised food grains from storage to every district. This strategy was formulated even before the national lockdown announcement (March, 2020) and enabled 2,356 Fair Price shops in 4,004 gram panchayats, 5,922 private shops, 2,034 SHGs networks and 69 Maitree shops with stringent social distancing norms.

Connectivity: Odisha's strong and well-established network of SHGs led by more than seven lakh women donned unorthodox leadership roles during the pandemic to not only keep the nutrition supply machinery going for the existing beneficiaries, but to reach out to almost all households of the state and spread awareness about the pandemic during the crucial initial days of the virus. They also supported community outreach efforts of the local administration in food supply.

In many networks, the SHGs had themselves undertaken delivery of cooked meals to senior citizens, differently-abled people, pregnant and lactating women and children under five years of age in the rural-tribal Odisha.

Coverage: Unlike many states, the Government of Odisha distinctively was able to cover maximum population including the migrant labourers into the state. Besides the food supply guarantee, the state actively distributed Rs 1,000 per ration card including new beneficiaries. The mid-day meal and TPDS supplies were strategically diverted towards volunteering kitchens.

Lessons from Odisha

Odisha faced the same pandemic that brought many a state government to a halt. While Odisha was being considerably ranked low in many indices at the national level, the most important feature of the state government during the pandemic time was the dynamic and evolving governance structure. It made efforts to strengthen community-based guidelines to tackle the burden of malnutrition at the grassroots level, through community health systems and by empowering local governance.

Its innovative and decisive approach towards problem solving by empowering community linkages and aligning resources behind it were the most basic yet effective policy intervention that other states could take a lesson from. However, admittedly district level disparities existed. More than 22 percent of Odisha's population is tribal, a population group with one of the highest rates of malnutrition and infant mortality rate.

The government drew up targeted interventions from within the existing schemes to address this issue.

3.6 Odisha's community radio stations' Yeoman service underscores medium's necessity in India

The state of Odisha has been a trendsetter on many fronts in the country's fight against COVID-19. But what has remained unsung is the role played by 17 Odisha-based community radio stations in this effort. It took me a pandemic to realise the yeoman service that they have rendered in 'reaching the unreached'. Low-cost yes, but not low on information, they have been catering to the information needs of communities in such remote locations where no mainstream print or electronic media reaches and worse, where even social media cannot reach due to absence of network to provide internet services. Equipped with a low power transmitter (50 watt), they are supposed to generate 60 percent of their content locally and in the local dialect, which uniquely positions them as the voice of the community.

When the coronavirus outbreak started in 2020, Radio Swayamshakti in Khariar, Nuapada, started a radio campaign to connect buyers with the milkman who had suddenly lost business due to lockdown. When the traditional media was publishing photographs of distressed milkmen pouring their unsold milk on the roads, this small but timely effort was changing things for the better.

Stations across the country came up with locally relevant jingles to promote wearing of masks, social distancing and hand washing in the local language and dialect of that region. Call centres were set up in the studios of the radios which not only broadcasted the frequently evolving guidelines as soon as they were announced, but also answered listeners' queries, thus providing an effective bridge between the community and the government in handling their grievances during the pandemic. They even went a step ahead in aiding the district administrations in supporting relief measures.

In Tamil Nadu, fishermen were starving since they had not gone to sea for almost one hundred days, firstly because of the ban and then due to the lockdown. Kadal Osai, a Rameswaram-based radio station promoted by social organisations, quickly connected the fishermen with Brittania and Muthoot Finance: Brittannia chipped in with Biscuit packets and Muthoot provided rations to them.

During the April 2017 riots in Bhadrak, Odisha, with fake news and misinformation further fueling the unrest, Radio Bulbul rose to the occasion with bulletins promoting peace and harmony. In Odisha's Nayagarh district, Daspalla-based Radio Surabhi's popular programme 'Suna Jhia' (Listen Girl or the Golden Girl) was a much-needed intervention in a district infamous for female foeticide. Other community radio stations have tackled varied issues like child marriage, sanitation, women empowerment, skill development, nutrition etc.

I did not even know that the Government of India's Department of Science and Technology had partnered with almost 400 stations to popularise mathematics in different communities. Besides, the Election Commission of India worked with 60 radio stations to create a voter awareness campaign on a pan-India basis during the run up to the 2019 general elections. There are close to 140 educational institutions and 22 Krishi Vigyan Kendras that are running community radios.

No other communication channel has been as expansively

effective as community radios during times of natural disasters. The Government of India came out with a Community Radio Policy followed by rules after they learnt that an illegal local radio in the sea coast saved a number of lives during the tsunami after it broadcast a timely warning to fishermen out at sea.

When Odisha battled Cyclone Fani, Konark's Radio Namaskar was broadcasting updates on wind speed and directions till its tower went down around midnight. Since electricity was shut down before noon, radio was the only source of information for the people on safer places to move to. Radio Ala in Kakinada, Andhra Pradesh is known for broadcasting weather reports for fishermen at sea, providing a valuable service during the regular onslaught of cyclones that the state suffers every year. Kadal Osai in Rameswaram works with the coast guard and marine police to aid rescue operations. There are around 30 stations in coastal India which work relentlessly during disasters.

Mainstream media, be it print or electronic, has largely been urban centric whereas India still lives in its villages. Further, in a state like Odisha where the tele-density is as low as 77 percent, meaning that about one-third of the total population and perhaps close to half the rural population do not have access to the internet, the community radio is the only medium that provides last mile connectivity. More importantly, communities can engage in two-way communication using these radio stations, thus fostering true community participation. Despite working in low-resource settings, community radios play an important role in advancing the unheard voices of the community. The administration could also use them for monitoring delivery of government programme, thus improving programme implementation. Most of the 267 operational community radios in the country are in rural areas, some in extremist areas and aspirational districts. There is, therefore, a compelling reason to make this movement more robust and expansive.

Yet, the government's policy, be it at the centre or the states, has not been very favourable to community radio stations. While GoI allows them to operate for a licensing fee, there has been little promotion of their schemes and programmes over these radios. District administrations seldom use them. Many state governments have not even evolved a radio policy till now. While FM stations with their huge urban presence are able to get advertisements from both government (Bureau of Communication, earlier called DAVP) and private sectors, community radios have not been so lucky. I am happy that I took up their cause with the Union Information and Public Relations Minister to recognise their potential and make community radio a revolution in India.

3.7 Odisha's 5T Agenda

Five 'Ts' propel Odisha's governance. They are transparency, teamwork, technology and timeliness — leading to transformation. The Naveen Patnaik government adopted the '5T' agenda to transform governance in all departments by bringing about big, transformational, institutional-level changes, and not incremental makeovers.

An effective public office is one that is transparent concerning its functions, expenditures, targets, tenders and contracts. It is also collaborative and communicative, leveraging the experience and skill of individual officers in the team. It uses technology to inform citizens, improve the delivery of services and receive their feedback. Such a governance system is, therefore, transformative for citizens. The 5T framework helps the government reduce information asymmetries existing in the society.

In sync with the 5T agenda, in October 2019, the government launched the 'Mo Sarkar' or 'My Government' initiative. Under this initiative, the phone number of every petitioner accessing a government office is made available to everyone in the system—the Chief Minister, ministers, chief secretary, secretaries and other responsible officers. The CM's office, at times the CM himself, and other officers make 10 random calls every day to such petitioners and get feedback on the quality of government services offered to them.

This process helps those who govern (the agent) obtain data on how government services function at the tail-end of the chain, at the point of contact with the people (principal). Here, the government can ascertain if the 'sub-agents' or bureaucracy can deliver on promised services such as basic healthcare or safety from crime, and immediately take remedial action in case of non-compliance.

Such a real-time feedback mechanism was always absent. Feedback was being collected through the bureaucratic hierarchy whose efficiency and effectiveness was sought to be assessed. This naturally led to a conflict of interest and prevented the 'agent' from receiving authentic feedback from the 'principal'. The Mo Sarkar effectively disrupts this state of affairs, allowing for power to shift away from the bureaucracy back to the people.

The Mo Sarkar is an 'action-based' feedback mechanism that utilises direct empirical evidence on performance at the de-centralised or operational level. This information contributes directly to improvement in the performance of the administration/bureaucracy and makes policy interventions and concomitant decision-making much more evidence-based, economical, efficient and effective. As a consequence, it also becomes more equitable and ethical.

To institutionalise it, the State has assigned weightage to performance under the 'Mo Sarkar' in the annual performance appraisal report of government employees. The government has already compulsorily retired sub-inspectors and suspended chief district medical officers and assistant engineers based on public feedback. In all, about 100 officers had either been compulsorily retired or terminated (from November 2019 to April 2020) under corruption charges and delinquency in delivering service to citizens.

The usefulness of the 5T framework was on full display in Odisha's fight against Covid-19. The action plan was known for swift and timely decision-making and efficient implementation. Some of the measures included automated registration system for foreign-returned Odiyas, tie-up with hotels as quarantine facilities, the partial lockdown of the State, the 1,000-bed Covid-19 hospital or the relief distribution to migrants holed up inside the State.

That said, there are some hurdles. The initiative relies on technology, but Odisha's teledensity, at 77.22 per cent, remains a significant constraint—the national average is 91.82 per cent. This should improve, particularly in the left-wing extremism affected areas where many villages have no access to mobile networks.

The 'Mo Sarkar' initiative has a Gandhian core. Mahatma Gandhi strongly felt that people are the real masters, and ministers, as representatives of the people, are their servants. The

5T-powered Mo Sarkar is to benefit the poorest and weakest among us, who desperately require the State and its agents to truly and effectively work for their benefit.

3.8 Odisha an example of growth for the country

Once a beleaguered backward region, Odisha now boasts of effective governance in partnership with panchayati raj institutions and uses a community-based response strategy towards combating crises.

The government led by the current chief minister came to power in the state in 1999 after the devastating effects of the super cyclone that had ravaged Odisha. The newly elected government rose to the occasion and thus began the transformation of Odisha to where it stands today. It is now known as the leader in natural disaster management by virtue of its immaculate preparedness and mitigation measures.

Contrary to the quintessential persona of politicians, the Odisha CM has been a silent and quiet performer. He has taken efforts to ensure a welfare state, be it via the rollout of the KALIA scheme for farmers, being vocal for adequate women representation in governing bodies, and organising and empowering women self-help groups.

The CM's action of distributing approximately 19,000 MT of liquid medical oxygen to 19 oxygen-deficit states when the country was facing a huge crisis during the second wave of Covid-19 in April-May 2021, has been applauded for the display of the true spirit of cooperative federalism. Some other standout achievements of the state include providing loans to landless farmers via the new institutional mechanism of a joint liability group, providing an assurance-based (as opposed to insurance-based) universal health coverage with special emphasis on women via the Biju Swasthya Kalyan Yojana, starting Adarsh Vidyalayas to foster education and announcing special packages for particularly vulnerable tribal groups in the state, to name a few.

Achievement orientation comes when basic needs are met: Renowned psychologist Abraham Maslow was the propagator of the 'Hierarchy of Needs' model wherein human requirements were ranked starting from the very basic ones of food, clothing and shelter to meeting higher-order aspirational and self-actualisation needs. The Odisha government ensured that the basic needs of its people were taken care of through a plethora of socio-economic welfare schemes. This led to enhancement in their capabilities and instilled in them the desire to move up the 'Hierarchy of Needs' ladder by looking for newer opportunities and aspiring to achieve them. The focus on achieving higher-order aspirations is slowly but certainly helping to unleash the true potential of the state and its people. Odisha's growth is also woven around skilling its people. This was recognised by the Europe India Foundation for Excellence as "Best State in Rural Skill Development" in 2019. The education and health sectors are also undergoing rapid transformation in the state. The larger plan is to make Odisha the education and health hub of the country.

How did Odisha achieve this feat? Governance in the state has been characterised by a 5T framework (an expanded version of the previously used 3T framework): technology and leveraging it, transparency in governance, team work from the various stakeholders involved and meeting targets in a time-bound manner, thereby leading to transformation. This nuanced approach of the government is the reason for the various accolades the state has garnered so far. The CM has not only catered to the basic needs via the Odisha Food Security scheme (SFSS) and Biju Pucca Ghar Yojana, but has gone miles ahead in making it an aspirational state despite its limited resources. Once a beleaguered backward region, it now boasts of effective governance in partnership with panchayati raj institutions and uses a community-based response strategy towards combating crises ranging from natural disasters to health emergencies such as the ongoing Covid-19 pandemic. What stands apart in all these initiatives is the involvement of the people to achieve community-level resilience and capacity to steer development.

The appreciation for Naveen's governance today, even by his most vehement critics, is a recognition of the fact that the CM will be long acknowledged as the premier leader in the making of modern Odisha. India must learn from the state on how to make the most of its available resources and dare to achieve the impossible.

3.9 Odisha's Lessons in Governance

'If you love your people, you don't fight for elections, you fight for change and transformation. If you work for the people, you will continue to live in the hearts of people like Mahatma Gandhi and Biju Babu. If you keep people at the forefront, it is not a political journey, it is a spiritual experience' – Naveen Patnaik

Odisha had for long suffered the humiliation of being showcased as one of the poorest in the country. But today it has taken the centre-stage in leading the nation by example, be it being the first city in the country to achieve clean drinking water from tap in the city of Puri or achieving hundred percent vaccination coverage against Covid-19 in Bhubaneshwar alongwith administering the first dose of the vaccine to one lakh migrant workers in the capital city. Needless to mention, it won full-some praise for its astute handling of both the first and the second waves of the Covid 19 by the internationally acclaimed Lancet journal. Adding to these champion acts, it recently garnered nation-wide appreciation for sponsoring the Indian men and women hockey teams whose sterling performances at the Tokyo Olympics 2021 made every Indian proud. It is the first state in the country that has officially sponsored both the teams since 2018 and has invested heavily in providing infrastructure, adequate facilities, organizing tournaments etc to the teams. In fact it is in the process of building the largest hockey stadium in Sundergarh, a district which has produced some of the most famous hockey players of the country, besides building astro-turfs in every block of that district to acclimatize players to usual playing conditions. What is even more laudable is the fact that when the national government or big corporates failed to sponsor them, Naveen Patnaik, heading a state government, stepped in. It was an eye-opener as to what genuine commitment and dedication can do to Indian sports.

Trajectory of Odisha's transformation

Disaster Management

The Naveen Patnaik led government came to power in the state in 2000 post the devastating super-cyclone of 1999 which had ravaged the entire State. The newly elected government rose to the occasion and thus began the transformation of the State to where it stands today. Today Odisha, a state which has faced more than 2 dozen severe natural disasters during the last 2 decades, is known as the leader in natural disaster management by virtue of its immaculate preparedness, mitigation and reconstruction measures. It has made the switch from being referred to as the 'disaster capital' of the country to getting two coastal villages as being 'Tsunami Ready' from the UNESCO-Intergovernmental Oceanographic Commission, making India the first country in the Indian Ocean region to demonstrate such high levels of disaster preparedness at the community level. It has also been applauded by the United Nations year after year for "strengthening disaster risk governance, investing in preparedness and scenario planning while spreading greater understanding of disaster risk." Odisha boasts of a Disaster Management Authority that dates back to the year 2000 when the country didn't have a national legislation and disaster management framework. The National Disaster Management Act of 2005 is largely modelled on these early works of Odisha. In 2018, Odisha became the first state in India to set up the sophisticated Early Warning Disaster Dispose System to resolve any existing gaps in the effective spread of disaster warnings through community resilience and minute by minute monitoring.

Women power

'Empowerment of women is the empowerment of nation. No household, no society, no state, no country has ever moved forward without empowering its women'- Naveen Patnaik

The Mission Shakti movement of Odisha, launched in 2001 involving seven million rural women has been organised into about six lakh women Self Help Groups (SHGs) who are provided financial assistance through extremely soft bank loans to encourage them to take up various self-employment works and micro-projects. Since 2019, Odisha has promised to dedicate Rs 5000 crore of marketing assistace to SHGs in the coming five years through government procurement systems such as PDS, midday meals and other nutrition support programmes besides medical supplies and infrastructure maintenance works. Women from these self-help groups also led from the front in Covid management and food distribution during the pandemic. Naveen Patnaik has also vehemently fought for political representation of women by giving his voice to the issue of women reservation time and again besides taking the first step in nominating one-third women candidates in the last parliamentary elections.

Transgenders Stand Tall

Also leading the nation by example, Odisha became the first state in the country to allow transgenders to apply to the state's police services thereby setting an exemplary precedent of inclusion of the LGBTQ+ community in state services.

Health for All in true sense

The State depicted true commitment of its 'Health for All' promise in the tactful handling of the several waves of the Covid-19 pandemic by execution of micro-containment and limited lockdown strategy coupled with erection of temporary medical facilities at Gram panchayat level with delegation of Collector's power to Sarpanchs, etc. Odisha's prodigious commitment towards health assurance and equity is also reflected in the Biju Swastytha Kalyan Yojana (BSKY) first introduced in 2018 and now strengthened and its ambit widened to provide a smart Health Card to more than 90% of all households of the State. Odisha is the first state to implement such a universal assurance-based health scheme. With this, the 4.5 crore population of Odisha can remarkably avail free healthcare services at all public health institutions irrespective of their income, status or residence. The health coverage provided under the BSKY is 30% more than what is envisioned under the PM-JAY. The annual cashless coverage of ₹5 lakh per family and ₹10 lakh per woman belonging to families from the economically weaker sections is a big step forward to bridging the existing health inequalities. The holistic design of BSKY to address systematic issues of healthcare in-accessibility of the BSKY goes over and beyond just insurance as in the Ayushman Bharat scheme where the bulk of the financial benefit accrues to the insurance companies. At a time when blood supply was an issue due to long periods of lockdown, Biju Janta Dal's Mo Parivar Jeevan Bindu, a programme that drew inspiration from Naveen Patnaik's call that "No one will face shortage of blood," successfully collected more than 1 lakh units of blood in about 10 months thereby setting a significant milestone for the state and an example for other political parties of the country.

Investment Destination

Odisha is also aiming towards making the state a haven for safe investments. In a major boost to the state's flagship "Make-in-Odisha," since November 2017, 195 industrial projects ranging across metal, renewable energy, textiles and food processing sectors etc with an investment value of Rs 92460.84 crore have been inaugurated. More than 60% of projects under Make-in-Odisha are in various stages of implementation. With the growth enabled by these projects, Odisha is emerging as the manufacturing hub of Eastern India. This has led to ever increasing flow of foreign direct investment proposals to the state even more than some of the traditionally well off states along with creating more avenues for jobs.

Poverty Reduction and food for all

The State has been successful in dropping its poverty levels by 25% over the past 20 years ever since Naveen Patnaik came into power. The State enacted the State Food Security Scheme (SFSS) to cover the people left out from the National Food Security Act (NFSA). The NFSA was aimed to cover 3,26,41,800 beneficiaries in Odisha which was only 78% of the 2011 census population leaving out close to 34 lakh people. To cover for all the people left out of the national scheme, the SFSS was enacted to ensure food security for all.

Urban Governance

Odisha is also a pioneer in urban governance. This is reflected in innovative and revolutionary schemes such as Jaga Mission. This mission is aimed at improving the living conditions in slums by transforming them into liveable areas equipped with basic services and civic necessities. So far, it has benefitted 1.8 million people living in 3000 slums. For its outstanding performance under this scheme, the state won United Nations' World Habitat Award 2019. This project was also conferred India Geospatial Excellence Award for using technology in transforming the lives of the urban poor. State's achievement in urban governance is also visible in other areas such as solid waste management, urban wage employment, water management, affordable housing, etc. Odisha won the Fastest Moving State in the Swachh Survekshan Awards 2020. In the latest India Smart City awards, Bhubaneshwar won 2 awards for its innovation in governance and citizen centric projects.

Agriculture

The State has several schemes in place for the upliftment of its farmers. While prioritizing the small and marginal farmers, the KALIA Scheme ensures income support through relieving debt-ridden farmers from their debt trap along with providing financial assistance to agriculture households, landless laborers, marginal cultivators of the state, and the elderly who cannot till their lands anymore. The State also provides loans to its landless farmers via a new institutional mechanism of Joint Liability Group (JLG). For its total food grain production, Odisha has bagged the Krishi Karman Award 5 times indicating the significant outcome of growth in its Agriculture sector.

Education

Odisha has begun work towards transformation of High Schools under the Mo School campaign by introduction of SMART classrooms, advanced learning aid, laboratories, and teachers' training programmes. Another effort towards holistic development of colleges is the launch of the Mo College Abhiyaan, drawing inspiration from the Mo School Abhiyaan whereby alumnis are linked to colleges thereby seeking their financial collaboration. Under this, the government has committed to contribute double the amount contributed by the alumni with a cap of 50L per year per institution. Odisha Adarsh Vidhyalaya, the brainchild of Naveen Patnaik, is another initiative to foster education in the State.

Financial Discipline

The economy of Odisha has registered tremendous growth trajectory since the year 2000. The average rate of growth in Odisha has been 7.5% which is higher than the national GDP average since 2012-13. In addition to that, the State has successfully maintained revenue surplus since 2015-16. Per Capita income of Odisha increased by 115.60% as compared to national per capita income which increased by 111.51% from 2011-12 to 2019-20 (RE).

How did Odisha achieve this feat?

Renowned psychologist, Abraham Maslow promulgated the famous 'hierarchy of needs' wherein human needs were hierarchically ranked starting from the very basic needs of food, clothing and shelter to meeting higher-order aspirational and self-actualization needs. The Naveen Patnaik led government ensured that the basic needs of its people were catered through a plethora of socio-economic welfare schemes which led to enhancement in their capabilities that went on to instill the desire of moving up the 'hierarchy of needs' ladder and thereby looking for newer opportunities. Odisha's style of governance is also driven by John Rawls's idea of justice wherein the state institutions ensure fair opportunity irrespective of social classes. Moreover, the policies are aligned to ensure maximum benefit of the marginalized groups based on the 'Empowerment Model'. As Prof Amartya Sen would say that growth happens when the capabilities of people are enhanced. The focus on achieving higher order aspirations is slowly but certainly leading to unleashing the true potential of the state and its people. This growth is getting woven around, in large measure. to skilling its people which got recognized by the Europe India Foundation for Excellence as "Best State in Rural Skill Development" in 2019.

Governance in Odisha has been characterised by a 5T framework (an expanded version of the earlier used 3T framework) which includes technological leveraging, transparency in governance, teamwork from the various stakeholders involved and meeting targets in a time-bound manner thereby leading to transformation. This nuanced approach of the Naveen Patnaik led government is the reason for the various accolades that the State so far has achieved. Corruption has also been specifically targeted under his governance with the mandated disclosure of assets right from the lowest officer in the government hierarchy to the Chief Minister himself. Odisha became the first state in the country to take such drastic measures to curb corruption in public departments.

Conclusion

Once a beleaguered backward State, Odisha now boosts effective governance in partnership with Panchayati Raj Institutions and community-based response strategy towards combating crises ranging from natural disasters to health emergencies including the recent management of the global pandemic. While rising to the highest tradition of cooperative federalism by supplying 19000 MT of the much sought after liquid oxygen to 19 states of the country during the second wave of the pandemic in April-May 2021, there is little doubt that Naveen Patnaik will be long acknowledged as the premier leader in the making of modern Odisha even by his most vehement critics. India must learn from Odisha how to make the most of its available resources and dare to achieve the impossible. Speak less, work more.

CHAPTER 4

DATA PROTECTION AND RIGHT TO PRIVACY

4.1 Right to life vs Right to privacy in Covid

In response to an alarming surge in Covid-19 patients, the Odisha government imposed a complete lockdown of 48 hours in three districts on April 3, 2020. The government took the decision to prevent the spectre of a community transmission of the disease. The State Government also disclosed the name and address of one out of about 40 positive patients (then) in Bhubaneswar who tested positive. The person's name was declared as he did not have a travel history, not even within India, and all attempts to trace his contacts proved unsuccessful.

The disclosure was aimed at calling upon all people who came in contact with this infected person, to self-identify themselves to enable contact tracing and restrict the spread of the virus. The disclosure of the patient's identity, however, drew criticism on the ground of breach of an individual's right to privacy. The criticism is particularly relevant now, when the country is discussing a new Personal Data Protection law and the government has asked people to download the Aarogya Setu application.

The Supreme Court in the *Justice KS Puttaswamy versus Union of India* case held that the right to privacy of an individual can only be subject to reasonable restrictions, when the restrictions are enforced through a law which pursues a legitimate state aim and are proportionate.

The disclosure of names of patients with the aim to trace contacts and stop the spread in such exceptional circumstances is a proportionate and necessary limitation to the person's right to privacy. Constitutional scrutiny of any government action related to Covid-19 must be contextualised within the extraordinary circumstances which inform such an action. Given the existential threat to the entire human race, it is imperative that the Union and state governments take all possible measures to map the transmission, identify potential carriers and prevent community transmission. We have seen the result of uncontrolled community transmission in countries such as Italy, Spain and the United States despite their admitted advanced healthcare systems.

Disclosure of the name of the patient was enforced by the state government through a law pursuing a legitimate state aim. On April 3, the government of Odisha had promulgated the Odisha Covid-19 Regulations, 2020, in exercise of powers conferred on it under the Epidemic Diseases Act, 1897.

The regulations strictly prohibit the disclosure of the name, address or telephone number of any person, except under 'exceptional circumstances affecting public health and safety'. The state government, in the instant case, disclosed the name of the patient under the above mentioned exception.

The restraint on the right to privacy of the concerned individual was proportionate as it was the least restrictive method available to the government to protect the public from the pandemic. The government had already failed in all its attempts to trace the infected person's contacts.

Reasonable restraint of the right to privacy of one person must be balanced against the right to life of an entire population under the well-settled doctrine of 'reasonable restriction' enshrined in Article 21 of the Constitution. The protection of the right to life and livelihoods of millions required that the right to privacy of some individuals is subject to reasonable restrictions as was resorted to in this case by the state government.

The disclosure of the details of only one person from among 40-odd positive cases then was not discriminatory as it was carried out under an exception well within the framework of law. The said exception satisfies the test of 'reasonable classification' and has a rational connect with the objective of protecting public health and safety.

Above all, let us not forget that law is 'for many, not the few'. A just society is one where the right of the individual is an instrument for the greater collective good, and not antithetical to it.

4.2 Need for an independent and robust Data Protection Authority

The Ministry of electronics and IT (MeitY)'s June 29, 2020 decision to block access to 59 Chinese mobile apps – by invoking the exception clause relating to sovereignty under Section 69 of the IT Act – has been welcomed by most, but it is at best an ad hoc measure. Amongst other concerns, the MeitY order specifically refers to the mining, profiling and unauthorised use of personal data. These issues are a continuing cause of concern for any application or data system and need to be addressed systemically and dynamically.

Ad hoc measures act at best as a temporary Band-Aid, but may result in disproportionate responses instead of well-planned alternatives backed by law and a well-defined strategy. The instant ban is yet another call for having a functionally robust Data Protection Authority (DPA).

The Personal Data Protection Bill, 2019 entrusts the DPA with the mammoth task of protecting the right to privacy of 1.3 billion Indians by regulating approximately 600 million entities including the proliferating digital ecosystem of both the government of India and the states. As opposed to a sectoral regulator like SEBI, IRDA, TRAI etc, the DPA is a sector agnostic body and has wide powers cutting across different sectors and economic spheres with powers to penalise not only both central and state governments but also other fourth branch watchdogs such as Comptroller and Auditor General of India and the Election Commission and even more significantly, the legislature and judiciary itself.

For impartial and effective discharge of its crucial role, there is a need for the DPA to have sufficient capability to discharge its functions. The EU shares its data only with countries which meet the 'adequacy requirement' under the General Data Protection Regulations (EUGDPR) and the OECD privacy guidelines. The independence of the DPA is the foremost criterion for meeting such a requirement and a necessary prerequisite for a free and fair cross-border transfer of data. Only with an independent DPA can India unlock its true potential in global digital commerce.

First, under the bill, the Centre has the power to notify

categories of 'sensitive personal data' in consultation with the DPA and concerned sectoral regulators. Such powers should vest solely with DPA as it is the primary rule making body under the bill and must remain at more than an arm's length from the government.

Second, the Centre is empowered under Section 86 of the bill to issue binding directions to the DPA without any prior consultation with it. This may adversely affect the functional autonomy of the body.

Third, while the power to notify certain large data fiduciaries as 'significant data fiduciaries' rests solely with the DPA, the Centre has been given the power (in consultation with the authority) to notify social media intermediaries as significant data fiduciaries, thereby diluting DPA's power.

Data fiduciaries at all levels of the government, ranging from the panchayat level to the Centre, will be regulated by the DPA. To design effective regulation, monitoring and enforcement mechanisms and create awareness of data protection rights at grassroots level, the DPA must be a decentralised body on the lines of the State Information Commissions or the Consumer Protection Authority and the Consumer Fora. A single centralised body as conceptualised may not even be able to functionally discharge its responsibilities of safeguarding every citizen's right to privacy and preventing any harm to him. Nevertheless, a decentralised body will pave the way for an efficient, agile and flexible DPA.

Further, given its cross-sectional mandate, the DPA may need to be constituted as a collegial body with a combination of full-time, part-time and independent members from judiciary, civil society and persons of ability, integrity and standing in the field of data protection, technology and regulation. Considering the brisk pace of change in the field of technology and data sciences, increasing DPA's capacity, both qualitatively and quantitatively, in this area is a crucial imperative.

The bill adopts good practices of involvement of various stakeholders such as industry, trade associations, various departments of the governments, other sectoral regulators and the public in the formulation of code of practices. However, the same transparent and consultative method is missing from the process of framing other rules and regulations. An opaque regulation making process has the potential of becoming the Achilles heel of the bill.

The DPA must also be required to publish results of inspections and inquiries that it conducts on data fiduciaries. Strong disclosure and reporting requirements must therefore be enshrined in the bill to gain the much-needed public trust and make enforcement effective. The DPA has to subject itself to the requirements under the RTI Act.

Lastly, the bill confers absolute discretion to the Centre for deciding the number of adjudicating officers, the manner and term of their appointment and jurisdiction. The adjudicating officers preside on disputes under the PDP Bill. This unfettered discretion may create issues of independence, conflict of interest and bias. The appointment of adjudicating officers must therefore be vested in an independent DPA with benches established at the district and block levels to improve accessibility.

Any law or policy is as good as its enforcement. Efficacious and effective implementation and enforcement depends upon capacity and capability. With rapidly progressing technology in a global world, we must envisage a DPA which is able to meet contemporary challenges, so that it becomes a model worth emulating.

4.3 Data protection regime needs to be robust

While the law seeks to strike a balance between privacy and public good, it vests too much power in the government.

The Personal Data Protection Bill, 2019 is on its way to becoming one of the first comprehensive pieces of legislation on data in the world. It aims to protect the fundamental right of privacy of citizens against excesses by both the State as well as private entities, including the powerful Big Tech companies like Google and Amazon and social media intermediaries such as Facebook, Twitter, etc.

This, however, is not the limited purpose of the Bill. The underlying objective of the legislation is transformative as it aims to recognise the value of data in promoting a free and fair digital economy even while keeping personal data of citizens secure and protected.

The report by the Committee of Experts, under the chairmanship of Justice Srikrishna, based on which the Government of India drafted the Bill, titled 'A Free and Fair Digital Economy—Protecting Privacy and Empowering Indians'. The Committee's report laid emphasis on providing equal importance to both the aims of the Bill, as is evident from the title and approach by the Committee.

An extract from the report summarises its approach: '(..) any regime that is serious about safeguarding personal data of the individual must aspire to the common public good of both a free and fair digital economy.'

Free and fair digital economy

The transformative objective of the Bill is also articulated in its Preamble, which states that 'it is necessary to create a collective culture that fosters a free and fair digital economy, respecting the informational privacy of individuals, and ensuring empowerment, progress and innovation through digital governance and inclusion.' Basically, the Committee and the Bill rightly realised the value of data in oiling the economy if used responsibly and purposefully.

Public good is often seen as a competing interest to the individual's right to privacy. A false trade-off between public interests of economic growth and data protection has often led a few cities to advocate for a narrow approach to the PDP Bill. However, practically, fundamental rights of individuals often go on to increase public goods.

This has found recognition in the Srikrishna Committee Report and the PDP Bill, where the individual is not treated as an atomised unit standing apart from the collective, but a part of it and their interests are inextricably linked. Rights to citizens empower the citizenry as a whole. Both the protection of personal data and facilitation of the growth of the digital economy serve a common constitutional objective of a free and fair digital economy.

As the report of the Committee notes, 'such an economy (free and fair) envisages a polity where the individual is autonomously deciding what to do with her personal data, entities are responsibly sharing such data and everyone is using data, which has immense potential for empowerment, in a manner that promotes overall welfare.'

In furtherance of promoting this notion of common

public good, the PDP Bill allows certain exemptions for data fiduciaries to share and use personal data of individuals in a manner that furthers the common public good.

First, in case of public health emergencies such as epidemics or disaster management measures, personal data can be processed and collected without consent of the data principal. The right to health of community over that of individual's informational privacy is given deference in the Bill.

Second, data collected for recruitment or termination of employment of a data principal by the data fiduciary is exempted from consent. This enables corporates and start-ups from being saddled with prohibitive costs of storage, maintenance and regulation, thereby facilitating ease of doing business.

Third, the Bill creates research exemptions, i.e., it exempts data used for archiving, research and statistical purpose from the full force of its provisions.

Fourth, for encouraging innovation in artificial intelligence, machine-learning or any other emerging technology in public interest, the Bill has provisions for creating regulatory sandboxes. Regulatory sandboxes permit limited regulatory exemptions so that companies can carry out tests and experiments without being overburdened with prohibitive initial compliance costs.

Fifth, the Bill also has exemptions for journalistic purposes subject, however, to compliance with any code of ethics issued by the Press Council of India or by any media self-regulatory organisation.

Sixth, manual data processing by small entities are largely exempted from provisions of the Bill to protect small and medium sector enterprises from undue hardships of compliance.

Seventh, the Bill allows exemptions to collection and

processing of personal data for legal proceedings, prosecution and investigations.

Lastly, the Bill enables the Central Government to be free to use anonymised or non-personal data for better targeting of public services and for formulation of evidence-based policies.

The way forward

Even though the Bill has taken strident steps towards achieving a free and fair digital economy, some issues remain unresolved. Blanket power to the Central Government to exempt itself or its agencies from any of the provisions of the Bill by way of an executive order needs a relook.

Similarly, the independence of the Data Protection Authority and adjudicatory authorities under the Bill are issues which require a deeper engagement. There is also over centralisation of powers into the Central Government, leading to stress in co-operative federalism. Further, there is an urgent need for a robust consent framework. Given the lack of digital awareness and literacy in India, one cannot presume that the consent given by citizens will be free and informed.

A truly transformative data protection regime in India must be one that empowers citizens and also limits governments' misuse of powers. Only with such a robust framework, India can confidently move towards the goal of becoming a leader in building a strong and robust digital economy.

4.4 Constitutionalizing Data Protection Authority

India's Data Protection Authority (DPA), as envisaged under the proposed Personal Data Protection (PDP) Bill, has been entrusted with the crucial responsibility of protecting and regulating the use of personal data of citizens.

The DPA is supposed to act as a bulwark against unconstitutional and illegal use of such personal data of citizens. Given its crucial role, the DPA is not merely an economic or sectoral regulator but plays the role of a 'fourth branch institution'.

However, the DPA lacks the independence of a fourth branch institution and does not have strong safeguards against executive and political interference or attempts at diluting its powers and functions with ease.

'Fourth branch' vs Sectoral Regulator

The constitution traditionally provides for three branches of state – the legislature, the executive and the judiciary. As the economy opened up, technical expertise became necessary. This gave rise to the proliferation of sectoral regulators such as the SEBI, IRDA, CCI or TRAI, which, while maintaining arm's length, would continue to shape policy and develop the nascent sector-specific markets in close co-ordination with the executive governments. These were statutory bodies created under an Act of Parliament, with the Central government having a large say in the appointment of its members, their conditions of service and removal.

Fourth branch institutions, on the other hand, play the crucial role of protecting core constitutional values such as democracy, transparency, impartiality, equality and equity, justice, freedom and human rights. They essentially have to maintain a character of complete aloofness, much beyond the arm's length, from the executive as they have to hold the executive to account in specified ways. They do not perform traditional executive functions of economic development or financial regulation but ensure horizontal accountability of the other branches of government. They are often constitutional bodies such as the Finance Commission (FC), Election Commission (EC) and the Comptroller and Auditor General.

Many bodies such as the Lokpal, Information Commission (IC) and the National Human Rights Commission (NHRC) have also been set up conceptually as fourth branch institutions with regard to their independence in functioning, but through statutes in Parliament.

The DPA has been entrusted the role of a fourth branch institution, primarily due to its overarching role in protecting the fundamental right to privacy of citizens against not only possible transgressions of such privacy by the private sector but also possibly by the government itself. As opposed to a sectoral regulator, it is a sector-agnostic body and has wide powers cutting across sectors and economic spheres. It is empowered to penalise both Central and state governments when they fail to protect an individual's personal data. In fact, it is also empowered to monitor sensitive data processed by other fourth branch watchdogs such as the CAG and the EC and even more significantly, the Legislature and Judiciary itself. As such, the DPA carries out crucial fourth branch oversight and accountability functions against almost all institutions of governance in our system.

Increasing independence of DPA

Why does the DPA lack the independence needed to be a strong fourth branch institution and ward off attempts of political interference?

This is primarily attributable to the fact that its structure and composition was inspired by sectoral regulators such as SEBI, IRDA and TRAI, based on the recommendation by the Financial Sector Legislative Reforms Commission as mentioned in the Justice B.N. Srikrishna committee report, 2018.

While the Srikrishna committee suggested inclusion of the Chief Justice of India or her nominee and one expert of repute in the Selection Committee, the PDP Bill introduced in Parliament provides for a committee comprising entirely of members from the executive, i.e. secretaries from departments of the Central government, without a judicial member and an expert. The power and discretion to remove any member of the DPA are vested with the Central government without a method or procedure for such removal being explicitly prescribed. The protection of the salary of the members has also been diluted and it shall now be prescribed by the Central government.

A DPA appointed solely by the Central government runs a severe risk of being in conflict with its purpose, interest and decisions while being called upon to take action against Central or state governments for possible breaches causing harm to some citizens, especially in large subsidy and health programmes run entirely by the government. Similarly, it may also adversely affect the federal structure of the constitution if it acts against the interests of state governments in a partisan manner.

The need for constitutional entrenchment

Thus, any data protection body must be largely independent, especially in the manner of appointment of its members, conditions of their service and the manner of their removal. They must not be appointees of the executive alone but must be appointed on the recommendation of a committee having bipartisan legislative representation and representatives from the judiciary – as is the case with the information commissions, the Central Vigilance Commission and the NHRC. Their removal from office must only be allowed in the same manner as a judge of the Supreme Court and their salary must also be fixed similar to the CAG or an Election Commissioner.

Only a constitutionally entrenched body will be sufficiently protected from executive aggrandisement, political control and institutional capture, leading to a robust fourth branch institution – one which can act as an effective guardrail against violation of the right to privacy. Incorporation of a full-fledged Data Protection Commission through a constitutional amendment must be envisaged by the legislature as a replacement for the DPA in its current form.

4.5 Data regulation in India must be reconsidered

Shortly after the Personal Data Protection (PDP) Bill, 2019, was formulated by the Government of India, the Committee of Experts on Non-Personal Data Governance Framework submitted its report. The Committee suggested a data policy blueprint for India, a country which 'can arguably be projected as being one of the top consumer markets and by extension data markets in the world.' Both the suggested regimes for personal and non-personal data regulation have adopted disparate models for regulation. To harmonise data regulation in India, there is a need for adopting a common overarching philosophy. Data regulation can broadly be classified into three categories—(i) privacy model, (ii) ownership model and (iii) the harm/accountability model.

The Supreme Court of India in *Justice KS Puttaswamy (Retd) & Anr. v. Union of India* (2017) adopted the 'privacy model' while declaring that the right to privacy includes personal data protection. In this model, a data market is not even conceptualised except in a very narrow sense as the overarching emphasis is on protecting the personal data of individuals. The Committee of Experts under the Chairmanship of Justice B N Srikrishna, which was constituted in pursuance of the Supreme Court's instructions, also adopted the privacy model in its report which was submitted on 27 July, 2018.

Privacy model

In the privacy model, data collection and processing by the data fiduciary are carried out only after consent of the data principal (unless in specific exceptions). Data is considered to be an extension of the private space of an individual and the individual's autonomy. Purpose limitation, use limitation and data minimisation are also subject to the consent of the data principal. Thus, it takes a rights-based approach. The PDP Bill follows this model. The European Union also follows this model in its General Data Protection Regulation.

Drawbacks of consent-based model

However, as some recent studies have shown, consent as a ground for data processing may become largely inconsequential as data principals are incapable of providing informed consent, especially in India due to lack of data awareness. Also, repetitive and long forms cause consent fatigue. Therefore, there is significant validity in the argument that data fiduciaries should not be allowed to absolve themselves of all liability for their future actions solely on the ground of the uninformed consent that they had initially obtained.

Further, in the emerging environment of big data and artificial intelligence, privacy principles of purpose limitation, limitation of use and data minimisation appear operationally not implementable. In fact, compliance with the privacy/consent model has caused heavy expenditure to private companies as well as the governments in European Union countries. The high compliance cost may be particularly harsh for small and medium entrepreneurs and stymie innovation and growth.

Ownership model

In the ownership model, data is considered to be property or an asset, thus making it amenable to marketisation and development of a veritable data market. Under this model, personal data derived from an individual and in its anonymitised form (which is then christened as non-personal data) will belong to the individual; whereas if data is produced by a source that relates to assets and processes that are privately-owned, it will belong to the entity that is producing the data.

The data includes derived, observed and inferred data that results from private effort involving application of algorithms and proprietary knowledge. Data generated from public efforts, i.e. collected or generated by the governments, or by any instrumentality of the governments, is classified as public data. The ownership model is a combination of both the 'data source' logic and 'data subject' logic, as opposed to the privacy model where the 'data subject' model is adopted. The Non-Personal Data Committee report suggests adoption of this model.

While this model can lead to the growth of a vibrant data

market, it may not be fit for personal data protection because granting of ownership rights to uninformed data principals may result in unintended harm to them due to the unpredictable nature of market forces. This is, however, the least-compliance-cost model from the perspective of data fiduciaries.

Accountability model

The third model for data protection law is the harm/accountability model, which requires that the data fiduciary will, notwithstanding the consent that it might have obtained from the data principal, continue to be liable for the harm caused to the latter as a consequence of its actions.

This model addresses the shortcomings of both the privacy and ownership models. On the one hand, it protects individuals from privacy harms irrespective of their uninformed consent. On the other hand, it also protects and acknowledges the proprietary knowledge and innovation put in by data fiduciaries to generate derived and inferred data. This again entails a high compliance cost for data fiduciaries, but is the least transactional. So the transaction cost is low.

Therefore, data regulation in India must be designed keeping in mind the 'harm/accountability model' to maintain a healthy balance between privacy rights of individuals and economic growth. This is critical to attain the objectives of the PDP Bill i.e. 'to create a collective culture that fosters a free and fair digital economy, respecting the informational privacy of individuals, and ensuring empowerment, progress and innovation through digital governance and inclusion.'

The 2019 version of the Bill in its design has turned out to be a hybrid between the consent (privacy) framework and the harm model, with the result that it has created a heavy compliance cost regime for both old and new data fiduciaries. This cost would become even more for data fiduciaries relying on legacy systems as there would be an added component of transition/migration costs. The non-personal data framework should also adopt the accountability framework so that the two become harmonious and integrated.

4.6 One data policy to protect privacy in India

The Committee of Experts on Non-Personal Data (NPD) released a revised report on the Draft Non-Personal Data Framework in July, 2020. The report attempts to provide a data policy blueprint for India, a country which 'can arguably be projected as being one of the top consumer markets, and by extension data markets in the world.'

Some of the underlying objectives behind regulating non-personal data is to tap into data as an economic asset, incentivise start-ups by correcting the imbalance established by a few dominant players and use data for public good and economic benefits of citizens while protecting collective community interests over such data as opposed to the personal data protection regime built in the Personal Data Protection (PDP) Bill that seeks to ensure primacy to the individual and not the community over his personal data.

To achieve these aims, the Committee has proposed a *sui generis* framework for non-personal data, independent from the personal data protection law. It aims to translate a category of data from 'club goods' into 'public goods'. Public goods such as clean air, street lights, drinking water, etc. have no rivals, are non-excludable and freely available. To avoid formation of possible monopolies in case of club goods, the committee identified key players and argues for establishment of a regime of rights and obligations.

Under the NPD framework, a 'data custodian' is the entity that collects, stores and processes non-personal data which may be a private entity such as a social media company or the Government itself. A 'data trustee', on the other hand, is an organisation which is responsible for handling of the non-personal data. A typical example would be a trade body such as NASSCOM.

A Data Trustee has the duty to seek all data from data custodians which 'may be useful for policy making, improving public service, devising public programs, infrastructures, etc.' These categories of non-personal data must be shared with other entities at no remuneration. The Committee puts these data in the category of what it calls as 'raw data'. However, similar terminology is absent in the PDP Bill. Besides, the PDP Bill defines 'data fiduciaries' as those who store as well as process data and 'consent managers' as those who would handle the consent of individuals.

The only exception to the overarching power of the data trustee to seek data from the data custodian are 'proprietary' or 'inferred' data (where insights are developed by combining different data points typically involving trade secrets, algorithms, computational techniques, advanced analytics etc).

While the PDP Bill makes no such separate categorisation of 'inferred data', it includes inferred data in the definition of personal data. Thus, inferred data could be either personal or non-personal. It is widely believed that making privately collected data available publicly may result in disclosure of business strategy as the pattern and nature of 'raw data' collected may reveal the direction of the business to its competitors. The Personal Data regulatory framework suggested under the PDP Bill however protects even the 'inferred' data.

Given the above conceptual distinction between both the regimes, the recommendation of the Committee to have an independent Non-Personal Data Protection Authority ('NPDA') notwithstanding the fact that there already exists a Data Protection Authority ('DPA') for regulating personal data and privacy may prima facie appear justified. According to the report, anonymised and non-identifiable data is regulated by the NPDA as non-personal data, whereas personal data is regulated by the DPA. It is however undisputed that data can never be fully anonymised and is always under the threat of re-identification.

Further, mixed data-sets in large volumes make it difficult for any authority to determine the anonymity accurately. Identifiable and anonymised data are not watertight compartments but a spectrum or a scatter. Data can exist at any point within the spectrum/scatter. Besides, which authority will decide if the data is identifiable or not? Thus, two authorities tasked with overlapping functions could be at loggerheads over jurisdiction thus creating unnecessary confusion and possible over- regulation. Hence, it makes eminent sense to harmonise both the regimes conceptually as well as in design and terminology which, to us, appears entirely feasible. A case in hand is the European Union GDPR which does not have separate regulations for PD and NPD. A common regime will lead to ease of compliance and reduction of regulatory costs, which will provide an impetus to businesses and economic growth. More importantly, it will enable the DPA to better protect community interests and privacy—by requiring data fiduciaries to take explicit consent from data principals, before they convert anonymised personal data into non-personal data. Further, a common framework will also enable harmonisation of regulation of data fiduciaries and data custodians—both of which are usually the same entity.

A single DPA will also allow resolution of a major point of conflict i.e., regulation of 'inferred data'. The committee, in fact, considered recommendations for consolidation of the DPA and NPDA but rejected it cursorily without considering the merits of the proposal at depth. The NPD report has successfully articulated a core philosophy of regulating non-personal data while at the same time increasing, public good. However, there is no compelling reason as to why the DPA cannot also be empowered to regulate non-personal data since Section 91 of the PDP Bill already regulates non-personal data for improving governance and growth. In fact, one of the aims of the PDP Bill (enunciated in its preamble) is 'to create a collective culture that fosters a free and fair digital economy, respecting the informational privacy of individuals, and ensuring empowerment, progress and innovation through digital governance and inclusion and for matters connected therewith or incidental thereto.' Thus, extending the Bill to non-personal data regulation only seems like a natural course of action. A single one can conveniently regulate both—efficiently and at a much lower cost.

4.7 Decentralizing Personal Data Protection Bill

The Supreme Court interpreted 'informational privacy' as a fundamental right derived from Articles 14, 19 and 21 of the Constitution of India, in *Puttaswamy vs Union of India* in August 2017. Hence, personal data protection is now guaranteed by the Constitution, not the central government.

Protection from whom

Basically, personal data is collected and processed by (i) state actors, i.e. central and state governments and their instrumentalities; (ii) non-state actors, i.e. private organisations providing services, social media intermediaries, e-commerce entities, big tech companies and employers; and (iii) other citizens.

The central and state governments are one of the largest data fiduciaries (who collect, hold and process data) in a wide array of state activities such as national security, welfare administration, subsidies, provision of municipal services and employment benefits etc. Similarly, in the age of big data, non-state data fiduciaries such as social media intermediaries like Facebook, Twitter, YouTube and giant e-commerce platforms also collect large amounts of personal data on a day-to-day basis. Citizens have also greater access to personal data of fellow citizens through the internet.

It's well-known that the maximum number of cases filed in the SC or high courts for infringement of citizens' fundamental rights is against the state. It is only recently that citizens have run to courts to enforce their privacy rights against big tech companies, e-commerce platforms and retail marketing corporations. Hence, it's quite likely that even in case of the proposed data law it is the state against which citizens would approach the courts for enforcement of their fundamental right of informational privacy.

Traditionally, fundamental rights adjudication has been

the domain of constitutional courts. With the proposed bill, a significant part of this judicial function, i.e. regulation of informational privacy of citizens, is proposed to be transferred to a Data Protection Authority (DPA). In the Justice Puttaswamy case, the SC instructed the government to pass a law which would regulate informational privacy not only from non-state actors but also from the state parties and other individuals.

Maintaining a balance between informational privacy and the development of a strong digital economy is a truly challenging task, requiring a qualified and neutral body at the helm. A core judicial task with the DPA would be to penalise governments and even suspend their operations when they fail to protect an individual's personal data.

In light of the critical adjudicatory role of the DPA to regulate not only private parties but also the central government itself, there's a necessity to set up a DPA independent of the central government which can implement the Personal Data Protection Bill in an unbiased manner. It cannot appear to be under the direct command and control of the central government.

The current design of the Bill gives a wide range of powers to the central government, as if it is the central government's responsibility alone to safeguard the informational privacy rights of citizens. For instance, the members of the DPA are appointed by a committee comprising officers of the central government instead of a judicial or bipartisan parliamentary body or panel. The design of the Bill effectively leads to central government regulating itself.

This design will also adversely affect the federal structure of the Constitution. For instance, a complaint filed against the

Chief Minister's Office for data breach will be decided by a body appointed by the central government as to whether such a breach took place or not and if held to be so, what would be the punishment or quantum of fine or other penalty.

Similarly, the Bill empowers the central government to decide if an event or incident arising in a remote location in a state is an issue of 'public order' or not and therefore, requiring 'exemptions' from application of the various safeguard conditions. This cannot be allowed as it creates fertile grounds for data hegemony by the Centre and a massive concern for federalism.

Comparable central overhang is seen in Sections 15, 33, 35, 44, 86 and 91 of the proposed Bill. Such powers should vest solely with an independent DPA which must be the primary rule making body under the Bill.

The DPA must therefore be established not as a regulatory body appointed by the central government but as a quasi-judicial independent body having judicial representation and should be subjected to only judicial oversight and monitoring and not executive supervision as envisaged in the current Bill.

On the same lines, there's an overarching need for a decentralised DPA structure with state bodies and bodies at the district level like the Consumer Protection regime and to a certain extent, the Right to Information regime. Mere copying and pasting the regime paradigms of the Competition Commission of India, or the TRAI or even the Income Tax and Central Excise or GST Appeal will not do. In fact, given the overarching and overwhelming role of the DPA as an umbrella regulator over the sectoral regulators, there is a greater need to make it not only independent and competent, but also efficient and effective.

It is important that the government heeds these

recommendations seriously. India can unlock its true digital potential as a data market only with an independent DPA, and not by a regime that irreparably harms our constitutional values and citizens' right to informational privacy.

4.8 Data Protection for minors in India

'The history of childhood is a nightmare from which we have only recently begun to awaken'. This observation made by de Mause, an investigator in psycho-histories in 2005 regarding traditions of child-rearing in different times and cultures, holds good for each age. He expounded that the evolution of child rearing gives insight into the development of a particular society. If this is the yardstick, what does that say about India's development when a mechanism to ensure data privacy of children is absent, while their presence online is normalised through formal government approval due to COVID induced physical meeting restrictions.

Enormity of the problem

As of 2019, the report of the Internet and Mobile Association of India noted that almost two-thirds of the internet users in India fall into the age brackets of 12-29 years. The report found that from a total number of 451 million monthly active internet users, over 66 million were in the age group of 5-11 years and 385 million were above the age of 12 years. The Puttaswamy Judgement in the year 2012 was categorical in stating that 'Privacy of children will require special protection not just in the context of the virtual world, but also the real world.' Eight years down the line, we have only begun to scratch the surface.

The OECD in the year 2010 released a report titled

'Typology of Risks Online.' These included three categories: Internet Technology Risks, Consumer Related Risks and Information Privacy and Security Risks. The grey area of Indian jurisprudence lies in mitigating the third risk which includes grave offences like targeted behavioural profiling, identity theft and intimidation of children online by misusing their personal data.

The Data Security Council of India noted that between the years 2016-2018, India had the second-highest number of cyber attacks. Two instances of a data breach in case of children set the stakes high and the alarm bells are ringing loud and fast. In September 2019, the personal data of 68,000 customers [mainly school-going children] of Vedantu was compromised and recently in May 2020, Unacademy reported that personal data of 22 million users has been compromised. The turning point in this discussion has now come in wake of the COVID-19 induced lockdowns. With education institutions shut, the best way to ensure continuity of education was bringing it online. Educational platforms like Byjus, Unacademy, Toppr, Edumarshal and the governments' Diksha have been widely used along with platforms such as Google Meets and Zoom to host virtual classrooms. So, the hitherto medium risks of harms to children have now multiplied several folds.

Current legal safeguards

The existing legislation that provides some degree of protection to children apart from the Juvenile Justice (Care and Protection) Act, 2015 is the Information Technology Act, 2000. These however do not entirely suffice. While the latter deals with the first and the second risk outlined by OECD, the former is only applicable to a select class of minors, i.e. a child in conflict with the law, a child victim, a child in need of care and child witnesses. The IT Act, when enacted in the year 2000, was done so as to 'legally recognise electronic transactions and facilitate e-commerce.' Further, the scheme of the Act mostly creates offences of wrongful disclosure and misuse of personal data in specific cases. The requirement of 'parental consent' and 'differentiated policies for children of various age groups' is absent within the Act. Thus, the act is insufficient to counter risks posed to minors on the internet concerning their personal data.

What needs to be done?

The UNICEF and the OECD Council have released principles to govern policies of states for data protection. The UNICEF in the 'Principles on Children Online Privacy and Freedom of Expression' has urged States to create mechanisms in relation to the evolving capacities of minors. On similar lines, the OECD also propounds for age-appropriate policies. With the General Data Protection Regulation, 2018 (GDPR) the EU urged members to have policies that require parental consent for those under the age of 13-16, along with safeguards such as 'child-friendly language for notices' and prohibiting 'sole decision making in use of children's data.' The United Kingdom obligates web-based applications to minimise data collection from minors and switch location services off by default. Under the US Children's Online Privacy Protection Act, 2000, the operators obtain consent from parents for the disclosure and use of personal information of minors. The South Korean 'Cinderella Law' forbids users under the age of 16, to access certain websites between midnight and 6 am.

Unfortunately, India does not have such mechanisms to protect children from online threats. As the personal Data Protection Bill is pending in the Parliament, in the meantime, the government must promulgate an ordinance or at least pass a regulation that guarantees some degree of safety to children. In 2020, the Supreme Court issued a notice to the Centre asking them to regulate minor's access to social media. While the above is a step in the right direction, it is time policy-makers act fast and carefully, especially given the current escalation in virtual education. The nudge has already come in the form of the report of the ad-hoc committee of the Rajya Sabha in January 2020 to study 'the alarming issue of pornography on social media and its effect on children and society as a whole,' in which I was a member.

4.9 Data Equity

The year 2020 saw the world go digital like never before, as a result of the pandemic that altered life as we knew it. The bright side of the past year was the spotlight on the significance of data and data flow. Taking the cue, the Government of India took important steps in tech policy and data regulation in 2020 namely non-personal data, health data, financial data, and data related to e-commerce etc. While the Personal Data Protection (PDP) Bill which was referred to a Joint Parliamentary Committee still awaits its final draft, in January 2021, the Non Personal data (NPD) Committee released a report shedding light on the types of NPD that may be collected, delving into public and private rights that may subsist in such data, as well as providing for a detailed data sharing mechanism that excludes transfers between private entities.

What is data equity?

Data equity is a broad term and incorporates an intricate and multifarious design. It focuses on the equitable deliberation of the ways in which data is assembled, scrutinized, evaluated, and distributed. Data equity can be classified into various facets of representation, access, feature and outcome. It reflects upon disparaged communities' uneven opportunities to access data and also the harm from the misuse of such data. It augments the question of data sovereignty, and the homogenization of data. Data equity urges us to consider the ways that data can stiffen stereotypes, aggravate concerns, or else subvert fair treatment. As they say, knowledge is power. Data as a manifestation of knowledge can create power asymmetry.

Who are the various stakeholders involved?

Data exchange encompasses individuals partaking in the exchange of their private information on the one hand and organizations/companies/social media intermediaries (SMIs)/ government on the other. What the pandemic revealed to us was a phenomenal digital awakening. In the past few years, we have had a revolution in the use of data and digital platforms for almost all of our needs. This highlights the need for data equity more than ever. For eg, a large part of the data that we share is personal in nature like location-specific, health-specific, work-specific, educational qualification specific, other personal details etc; to ensure that this information is efficiently utilized, the laws must work around a mechanism that ensures that this data is managed in a way that insures representation equity, access equity, outcome equity and feature equity. Structural inequalities have plagued our governance for years. Decision making based on biased data can further fortify and validate prejudices. As we advance towards this era of digitalization, it is imperative we recognize these inequalities and ensure that the digital space is devoid of them.

Why must we focus on the need for data equity?

The escalating accessibility of digital data mirrors the economic and human development, and specifically the accessibility of data emitted as an offshoot of the use of technological devices and services by the masses; it has both political and practical connotations for the way people are perceived and managed by the state and by the private sector. However, the data revolution is so far predominantly a technical one. The threat is that data-driven discrimination is advancing at a similar pace to data processing technologies, but sadly awareness and mechanisms for combating it are not. There is a need to put together a mechanism whereby there is transparency in the way people are made visible, represented and treated as a result of the data advanced by them.

The idea of data equity integrates a myriad of approaches, disciplines and concerns.

Firstly, as a part of an emerging debate, data equity has given rise to divergent interpretations of the interplay between data and social justice, and to distinct strategies and responses. Very often, data equity could be perceived as a response to the societal implications of data-driven technologies that have tended to address issues like efficiency, security, privacy and data protection. The infamous data breach by Facebook-Cambridge Analytica of the personal information of close to 50 million people which was later used for political advocacy was an eye-opener to the need for equitable data laws.

Secondly, the fabric of data equity widens the terms of the debate in a way that combats a myriad of issues that are compounded in the data-fied society, for eg. the embedding and introduction of disparities, decision making powered by biased data leading to bigotry and ostracism of certain groups, disintegrating working conditions, or the dehumanisation of decision-making and interaction around susceptible issues.

Thirdly, this discourse pushes the digital infrastructure to engage more categorically with questions of inclusion power, and politics, in addition to established notions of principles, sovereignty, trust, accountability, governance and citizenship.

Lastly, discourse on data equity has emerged at the intersection of activism and technology in which data is looked at as an avenue to revert or challenge dominant understandings of the world, social justice claims to transpire and (re)fabricating avenues for counter-imaginaries.

Conclusion

Data has taken centre stage in world economies which stems the threat of privacy violation and biased governance. Government framework around data management is already devoid of trust as was clear in the public outrage against AADHAAR biometrics case and the contact tracing feature of the Aarogya Setu app. We should use data equity as a form of critique, a blueprint of how data-driven developments should counter social justice concerns and age-old struggles against inequality, suppression and abuse. Ensuring data equity serves as a prolific avenue to seek reforms that can better endorse impartiality and justice. If data is not made equitable, it would be counterproductive to digitalization. To conclude, data equity can advance principles and practices to smooth out processes that may lead to exemplary results. The objective of data equity in this sense, therefore, is to identify where and how changes in data developments need to come about. Trust building is paramount. Since India is still in the stage of developing its data protection laws it must work towards ensuring data equity in its PDP and NDP laws.

4.10 Data Quality Governance

Data has rightly been dubbed as the new oil and has changed the world we live in. Indispensable as evidence in the realm of public policy, strategies and achievements for various governance outcomes are increasingly being driven by data analytics. Today, India in general and Odisha, in particular, has been able to manage its cyclones much more effectively with almost zero loss of lives largely due to precise monitoring of the cyclone path by the Indian Meteorological Department (IMD) and almost accurate forecast of the place and time of land fall besides wind speed and other parameters. This has allowed the governments to adopt proactive preparedness and mitigation measures besides post-disaster incidents response and relief instead of a reactive emergency response. But the accuracy of models is dependent on the accuracy of data which, in this case, is ensured by automatic capture of atmosphere data through sensors rather than through manual methods. Thus, data quality alone can improve evidence-based planning, implementation, monitoring and overall governance. Use of artificial intelligence, machine learning and big data analytics on inaccurate data sets can generate only inaccurate forecast models resulting in poor and misdirected policy making and implementation. The COVID-19 pandemic has been a dreadful reminder of this. Delayed and inaccurate data capture leading to inaccurate modeling about the timing and intensity of the spread of the virus may have cost us human lives. Similar concerns about data quality have also been raised in our economic data sets, consumption and employment data sets and even on our census data.

The Bad Data Crisis

The characteristics of good quality data are accuracy, completeness, reliability, relevance and timeliness. Such data is reflective of the real-world situation and can forecast the future course of various indicators with remarkable ease. Improving the situational knowledge of a crisis through accurate, timely, complete, relevant and continuous collection of data has changed the way policymakers operate in crisis management and disaster preparedness and mitigation.

The risks involved with using bad data for analytics and modeling are too many. It comes at a huge cost and compromises civic rights, ultimately leading to bad decision making, under performance and poor governance. Thus, data quality must no longer be compromised, especially in high-stake situations like the COVID-19 pandemic. Across the world, policy responses to the crisis have relied on data sets such as the number of tests, the number of positive cases and the daily death toll to understand the spread of the virus and its nature. Through statistical computation methods, forecasting models have been generated that predict the waves of COVID-19, its peak and the fatality rate. These models have facilitated targeted government interventions and geo-specific emergency response measures. However, the data culture in India is riddled with age-old bureaucratic ways that compromise data quality. The absence of data both of migrants during the first lockdown and deaths due to the lack of oxygen illustrates its narrow scope. Post the second wave, India also observed instances of delay in reporting of COVID-19 deaths along with the phenomena of adding backlog deaths to the official state figures weeks later due to time taken for audits to be computed. All this leads to poor modeling and hence, the inability to predict the actual scale and intensity of the next likely wave.

Audits have been undertaken late and have continued updating databases late. Such data gaps along with a poor reporting system are of grave concern. Besides delays due to audit, what is even more problematic is that the system to capture the initial data in villages and panchayats, may not be robust even under usual circumstances.

With the number of fatalities suddenly increasing manifold in the villages due to the pandemic, the figures are likely to have been captured inaccurately everywhere, particularly where deaths didn't take place in hospitals. The National Guidelines for Data Quality in Surveys issued by National Data Quality Forum (NDQF) along with the Indian Council of Medical Research and National Institute of Medical Statistics (ICMR-NIMS) recommends essential checklists and advance monitoring of data quality.

Though this is a step in the right direction for overall improvement of data quality on health indicators, it is not sufficient as all protocols related to data governance and its eco-systems need to be made more robust.

Way Forward

The first step for a systematic data quality strategy requires capturing accurate data. For holistic and complete data sets, accurate data must be captured at the village, panchayat, district, state and national level. Of these, primary data to be captured at the village and Panchayat level is of utmost importance and significance. Employing the latest technological tools is most crucial for capturing and collecting data, as the chances of contamination are highest here.

Therefore, data must be collected directly from its primary location where it is in its most sacrosanct form. Such a clean process of data collection is rid of ambiguities and misaligned objectives that aids strategic decision making with precision. The second step is to form a task force for data quality governance where the states are a party. Such standardized data architectures encompassing not only data capture, but ensuring integrity, completeness, validity, reliability and timeliness of such data to be captured, if adopted, can remove inadequacies from its subsequent use in policy and governance by using latest data analytics tools like machine learning and artificial intelligence etc. As public policy increasingly becomes data-driven and evidence-based, a rich data culture, a complementary data eco-system and data governance are imminent needs. Proper and qualitative data governance in an integrated digital system with multiple stakeholders can systematically and fundamentally address public concerns of privacy and data security also.

4.11 Challenges of Data localisation and the way forward

Over the last couple of years, data localisation has become a hotly debated issue right from the time the Reserve Bank of India came out with its notification mandating 'storage of payment system data' within India. Subsequently, the proposed Personal Data Protection (PDP) Bill, 2019, also envisages a graded localisation regime for different categories of data.

While these regulative measures can be seen as 'push' options, Finance Minister Nirmala Sitharaman's 2020-21 Budget announcements incentivising the private sector to set up data centres/parks across the country is an effort at 'pulling' entrepreneurs to develop an Indian market on data storage and processing, much in the same way as in the West. The issue is likely to gain fresh thrust in light of PM Narendra Modi's recent call for Atmanirbharta (self-reliance) as a measure to revive the economy in a post Covid-19 world. Together, these developments have the potential to propel the growth of India's data storage and processing industry significantly, by unlocking new opportunities for domestic businesses.

On the flipside, studies have pointed out some possible adverse impacts of mandating data localisation by law (hard regulation) and/or disconnecting from global value chains and the impact on multiple stakeholders including MSMEs. Hence, a cautious approach needs to be followed. Problem areas: While data localisation may facilitate growth of data centres in India, along with its positive impact on national security, economic development, etc., a study by Consumer Unity & Trust Society (CUTS), a think tank, on consumer impact assessment of data localisation found that it may have an adverse impact on freedom of speech, privacy violations, data breaches and cyber-attacks, and most importantly on innovation.

This is largely due to an inadequate data security regime and data breach laws, weak compensation regime for data breaches and high compliance costs, particularly for MSMEs, start-ups, etc. Another CUTS study found that data localisation may have an adverse impact on India's digital services export. One of the major factors behind India becoming a world leader in digital services export is uninterrupted flow of data across borders and favourable policies. Data localisation may add a regulatory compliance cost to the companies, particularly the MSMEs, and hinder the participation of domestic start-ups in global value chains, thereby affecting foreign investment and innovation in the country. In the PDP Bill, data has been categorised into personal, sensitive and critical data.

While there is no restriction on processing or storage of personal data, sensitive data must be mirrored in India and can be processed outside India. Critical personal data cannot, however, be processed or stored outside India though what is critical personal data has not been defined in the Bill and has been left to the Centre to notify later. This has brought the spectre of surveillance on citizens not just by government but even by foreign agencies and social intermediary data fiduciaries. Though the country is generating enormous amounts of data, it does not have the capacity to store them within its territory under the data localisation mandate and has a long way to go with regard to the availability of data centres in comparison to developed countries as well as its peers in the Asia-Pacific region.

Need a balanced approach

We have to understand that the data economy is a sunrise sector in India. Our data consumption has been rapidly increasing over the last few years. For example, within a month of the imposition of a countrywide lockdown due to the Covid-19 pandemic, data consumption in rural India witnessed an almost 100% jump. With an evident growth in data generation from increased business transactions through electronic means and supplemented by data localisation policies and laws, it is time to incentivise local private players to establish data centres in India rather than creating a hard regulations regime. We should adopt a 'regulatory sandbox' approach including regulatory impact assessment.

By 2024, the data centre market in India is expected to generate revenue worth $4 billion. In order to handle this increasing data volume from data localisation, India would need to ramp up its data centres capacity by at least 15 times over the next seven to eight years. Though investments are coming in, there is still a need to remove regulatory hindrances. As much as 60 different permits are needed to establish data centres in India, which span 15 government departments. Similarly, issues such as uninterrupted power supply, quality and availability of brick and mortar infrastructure in land banks, expensive real estate and networking components also act as roadblocks.

The announcement in 2020 by the PM of bringing in an ecosystem of 'plug and play' is the way forward. It is important to understand that along with ensuring data access to law enforcement agencies for providing security as a public good and securing data of Indian citizens from foreign surveillance, the government's move towards data localisation may be seen as a decisive and robust step towards making India the data services capital of the world by providing cheaper and more efficient options to corporates, banks and multinationals. It would help generate employment opportunities, and spur domestic innovation.

4.12 Need for surveillance law beyond data protection

A large part of the effort between the Union and state governments in contact tracing, widespread testing, disease surveillance and quarantining was coordinated under the Integrated Disease Surveillance Project (IDSP), the decentralised state-based disease surveillance programme established in 2004 with the National Centre for Disease Control (NCDC) as its nodal agency.

The IDSP is operationalised by state governments through a strong network of health workers, who collect and compile patient data to monitor, detect and respond to epidemics. This is largely done manually. Similarly, the Aarogya Setu mobile app was also at the forefront of government responses in identifying clusters and hotspots.

An efficacious government surveillance programme requires collection and processing of large scale personal data, including sensitive health and location data. This has raised crucial concerns relating to protection and privacy of the personal data so collected and the purpose for which it would be used after the pandemic is over. Recognising that data privacy is a part of right to life and a fundamental human right, the Supreme Court has already comprehensively enunciated the principles of informational privacy and data protection in its celebrated judgment of *K.S. Puttaswamy vs Union of India*, which has also found articulation in the Personal Data

Protection Bill, 2019 (PDP Bill) currently under discussion in a joint parliamentary committee of which I am a member. The committee submitted its report on 16th December, 2021.

Some of these principles include reasonable processing of data, purpose limitation, collection limitation, lawful processing, storage limitation, data quality and accountability along with crucial rights of persons whose data is being collected. One such right is the right to be forgotten. Once enacted, collection and processing of the personal data – both by government, corporate and non-government organisations – will be subject to the provisions of this PDP Bill.

Two questions then arise for consideration. Firstly, what measures should be taken to protect the personal data of citizens until the PDP Bill is enacted as law? And secondly, is there a need to enact a separate umbrella surveillance law or make separate sectoral laws?

It is important to note that both the IDSP and Aarogya Setu are operating in a legislative void. There is no overarching surveillance law either, even in the matter of national security where the protocols for data collection and surveillance have been laid out merely in executive orders. A protocol for Aarogya Setu was released in 2020 by the Ministry of Electronics and Information Technology, but the same does not provide for a legislative foundation.

On the one hand, the protection of personal data has been recognised as a fundamental right, while on the other, there is an absence of law to effectively outline the state purpose in collecting such data and enforce, limit and balance the rights of citizens against the larger public interests. The Epidemic Disease Act, 1897 or the Disaster Management Act, 2005 by the government does not address these concerns at all. Therefore, a law sanctioning collection of data and requiring the government to follow crucial data protection and surveillance principles is the need of the hour.

One surveillance law or several sectoral laws?

The next question is whether there should be several sectoral laws setting out separate mechanisms of data protection and surveillance principles in each sector or an umbrella surveillance law. The PDP Bill enumerates the principles of data protection, as well as provides for mechanisms to address any violations of its provisions.

For example, the 2019 Bill imposes fines on a corporate or person when they fail to comply with certain provisions of the Bill. Similarly, it also provides for an adjudicatory mechanism where the citizens may seek compensation for any 'harm' caused to them due to the violation of any provision of the Bill. However, in order to detect and determine breaches in the data protection and processing principles (such as purpose limitation, collection limitation and storage limitation), there must be a clear enunciation of the purpose and use of such personal data within a legislative framework. While an umbrella law may be simpler and easier to frame, it may miss out sector specific nuances to achieve the stated state purpose.

For example, collection of data and its use to achieve the state objectives would be different in case of the health sector as in case of the current pandemic from that of the security of the nation considerations involving issues of terrorism and counterfeit currency. The surveillance requirements in both cases would understandably be different. It can be carried out best by the industry-specific regulator or the appropriate ministry having a detailed understanding and knowledge of the sector. Only such a specialised approach can lead to an effective formulation of the purpose, use and necessity of personal data for specific purposes and an effective adjudication of the violation of data principles under the PDP Bill, 2019.

CHAPTER 5

TECHNOLOGY AND ARTIFICIAL INTELLIGENCE

5.1 Consumers' trust is a must for Artificial Intelligence

Artificial Intelligence (AI), believed to be the most important innovation after electricity, is an integral part of the Fourth Industrial Revolution (4IR). While the global AI market rose by 154% in 2019. By 2021, it was predicted that 80% of emerging technologies will be based on AI.

Benefits of AI adoption

AI is closely linked with consumer welfare. Consumers are greatly benefited when AI drives innovation to provide novel interactive applications using facial and voice recognition, speech to text as well as text to speech conversions, virtual assistants, etc. to improve the user experience of availing products and services through price/product comparison tools and tailored products/services. It also maximises efficiency by reducing information asymmetry between the buyer and the seller and optimizes price discovery, thus, leading to wider consumer choice, and better availability/access to products/

services. In addition, it enhances convenience by enabling smart appliances/machines, such as robotic lawnmowers and vacuum cleaners, smart plan watering systems, and other smart home appliances. It is also known to be having the potential to drive effective delivery of public services, such as those pertaining to healthcare and education, among others. For instance, AI is being extensively used in finding public health solutions for Covid-19, including drugs and vaccines, apart from its use in tracking and tracing.

Problems in the adoption of AI

However, consumers also bear the brunt of its misuse. Firstly, AI systems rely on processing big data sets, which contain a mix of personal data, sensitive personal data, community data, and non-personal data. Many times, such data is prone to breaches and privacy violations. In the Personal Data Protection Bill, 2019 (despite having its many demerits), there exists a void in regulations governing non-personal data and community data.

Secondly, AI systems are only as good as the data they process. Biased data sets on grounds of race, gender, income, etc. are known to lead to biased AI decision-making leading to discrimination and prejudice towards a certain class of consumers.

Thirdly, AI has the potential to enable businesses to ascertain consumers' willingness to pay for a given product/service. This may lead to price discrimination, through dynamic pricing, thereby adversely impacting consumer welfare. Also, businesses, empowered with AI, can assess consumer preferences and behaviour to orchestrate personalised advertisements, offers, and inducements, which although sometimes beneficial for consumers, can also lead to unduly influencing the choices and reactions of the consumers. This may lead to consumers losing absolute control over their purchase decisions.

Lastly, there are also risks of market collusion (tacitly) between close competitors, leading to loss of choice and higher prices for consumers by the violation of competition laws.

These risks arise because while AI makes predictions for consumers based on their data, but it functions within a 'black box'. This 'black box' creates information asymmetry for consumers in understanding the processes and design of AI mechanisms through which these technologies come to a decision. For example, a consumer might not be able to trust an AI-driven diagnostic tool as it lacks the assurance factor compared to when the same diagnosis is performed by a medical practitioner.

Taken together, such risks are likely to dent consumer trust on AI-driven products/services. The individual need not be afraid of using AI and in fact, need to have more confidence in AI to ease his living. For this, consumers must be kept at the centre of any policy or regulation on AI, including mandatory consultation with consumers in policy/regulation-making processes to win their trust in the emerging ecosystem.

Regulation of AI to build consumer trust

Hence, there is a need to regulate the adoption and use of AI. But the regulations need to match the pace of the dynamically evolving AI-driven digital technology, particularly since the adoption of AI in India is in its infancy. Regulations must be evidence-based and ensure that costs imposed by proposed regulations do not outweigh the intended benefits. There should be optimal regulations, wherein innovation is encouraged, while also enhancing consumer welfare through protection from its allied risks. Thus, light-touch regulations with elements of self-regulation have to be encouraged.

India immediately requires a data protection law that can manage the potential negative externalities arising from the use of AI and ensure individual privacy. A robust competition policy would also be helpful in minimizing risks. There is already a consumer oversight mechanism prescribed under the Consumer Protection Act (2019) to provide adequate consumer redress. This oversight mechanism as also the data protection regime should have the structural and functional wherewithal to test any AI technology for trust, fairness, accountability, and transparency. Further, it should be actively educating the consumers about AI processes so that information asymmetry between consumers and the seller is reduced.

Conclusion

On top of all these regulations imposed on businesses, businesses will also need to ensure ethical use of AI and be transparent with their business practices. Else they would not only face the sword of hard regulation in the form of full government control but may also lose consumers' trust. Ethical use of AI can also be promoted through creating impact assessment tools that can measure the effect of AI through a trust index as done in the UK. This will help build more ethical and human-centred AI systems.

5.2 Building a robust AI Landscape in the country

In December 2018, the Government of India approved the Rs 3,660 crore national mission on cyber-physical system technologies: artificial intelligence (AI), internet of things (IoT), machine learning (ML), deep learning, big data analytics, robotics, quantum computing, quantum communication, quantum encryption, data science and predictive analytics.

Earlier the same year, NITI Aayog had published the National Strategy for Artificial Intelligence discourse paper, which recommended setting up an AI Research, Analytics and knowledge Assimilation (AIRAWAT) platform. Meanwhile, the government had also constituted four committees on AI in four well-considered areas. These committees have since submitted their reports to the government; they are available on the MeiTY website for public comments.

India is gradually adopting artificial intelligence into its system. Indian start-ups and unicorns have been deploying AI tools for better delivery of services. Many of the recent initiatives of the government, whether the Aarogya Setu app or the MyGov application, aim at the use of AI to make world class products. However, we are still miles away from unlocking the true value of the huge repository of data collected from different sources using AI and ML techniques, in both the government and the private sector.

Improving diffusion of AI

There are two broad requirements for diffusion: policy push for spread of AI adoption, and trust of consumers or users, which is the 'policy pull'. The policy push has been inadequate. The other key ingredient of diffusion is to gain the trust of consumers and citizens by protecting their privacy and data, which is again missing due to the absence of a privacy law in India.

First, there has to be increased long-term investment in AI in both the public and private sectors. India lags behind the top five geographies for private sector investment in AI. The US is far ahead, with investments worth $18 billion, followed by Europe ($2.6 billion) and Israel ($1.8 billion). According to one estimate, China accounted for a greater share of global private-sector funding than the US. Large companies can afford to invest in R&D but only a few are venturing into it; they are either scared, being risk averse, or are slow. The start-ups don't have the money to invest in developing AI and are facing capacity issues. Accordingly, they prefer using existing models rather than develop new ones.

Second, the scope of using AI and block-chain to unlock efficiencies of organisations and systems is at its maximum in our public sector and government departments. To boost AI infrastructure in India, there is an urgent need for government departments both at the Central and the state levels to adopt AI-based solutions to solve the legacy and intractable problems being faced by them – from increasing agricultural productivity to climate change, from air pollution to disaster management. This will have a multiplier effect that could spur the private sector to jump in.

Third, the government and the private sector must work hand-in-hand, particularly on the R&D aspects of AI. Public-private partnership models bringing together the expertise of research institutions and universities (including the institutions of eminence), market knowledge along with financial skin-in-the-game by the corporations and partial financial grants by the government will inspire confidence to innovate using AI. The involvement of the private sector could ensure the research output is market-competitive.

Fourth, promoting STEM courses in early education, revisiting the course-curriculum in colleges and on-boarding industry experts to teach final year students were some of the key recommendations by a tech policy think-tank, The Dialogue, sometime back. Indian higher education programmes also need to be tweaked to include training on AI that cuts across disciplines. The vast network of hugely successful and talented Indian-origin professionals heading large multi-national corporations abroad must be utilised to institutionalise knowledge-sharing, mentoring and collaborative R&D initiatives.

Fifth, a fundamental challenge with regards to the development of AI in India is the quality of connectivity in the country. India needs to work towards improving its infrastructure and thereby allow for an environment that supports the growth of new technology.

Last, because AI is so powerful as it has all the information about a consumer to potentially be able to manipulate their behaviour, choices and preferences, India immediately requires a data protection law to ensure individual privacy.

AI is the future that India can ill-afford to ignore to solve some of the most intractable problems of its people. Fortunately, it has potential in its labour force, academic institutions and geopolitical status. If recognised and used correctly, India can become a leader in AI development. Further, indigenous innovation can be incentivised by creating a 'Central Innovation Fund' accessible to both the central and the state Governments to propagate AI in different sectors.

In order to guide India's AI missions, we may also like to create a body like Indian Space Research Organisation, which has successfully guided India's space missions with a high degree of self-reliance. Thus far, the sectoral approach has led to an arguably silo-type approach towards AI, which must be replaced with a whole-government approach like that of Singapore to foster a holistic and trustworthy AI ecosystem in India.

5.3 How well can India use Blockchain?

Blockchain technology has emerged as a significant transformative force in India in multiple aspects of governance, more particularly in private sector operations. However, its adoption in government leaves much to be desired.

Though its potential has been recognised in reducing operational costs and compliance charges as well as in improving efficiency worldwide, the failure of governments in India to usher in its adoption both at the central and state level is inexplicable. It has remained largely in the private sector space until now.

Here I list some of the most significant possible useful cases of blockchain technology for India.

Storing Health Data

Blockchain holds the power to completely transform the healthcare system by carefully consolidating the health data of a person together by storing the data separately in different distributed ledger like databases for security purposes.

The person can share this information as and when the need arises. This will help in providing freedom of movement within the healthcare system as a patient moves from one hospital to another without undergoing on-boarding procedures.

Meanwhile, medical professionals can also access the medical history of the patient immediately, thus saving time and making the whole process more economical as well as efficient. Fraudulent access to such data is also almost impossible. This is achievable by creating Electronic Health Records (EHRs).

Furthermore, introduction of digital prescriptions can save people from the burden of visiting the doctor every time the prescription expires.

Securing Land Registration

It has been established that by using blockchain technology, the government can remove intermediaries and connect directly with citizens.

Land registration and land titling is an area that requires a plethora of document verifications, along with transparent records of a number of transactions. There are often complaints of fraudulent transactions in this space where criminals allegedly use fake identities for verification purposes which often takes a long time. This entire operation can also be up-scaled to include a wallet service with nodes that store public and private keys.

These keys can create a unique signature or multiple signatures to initiate a transaction in the system thereby removing the need for third-party verification.

In a land registry process, this would ensure a reduced need for officers in land offices to do title or deed searches (to certify non-encumbrance) or land registrars to verify document contents and update the registry.

The cryptographic protocols embedded in this distributed system can secure the network as well as the transactions and ensure data privacy. Additionally, transactions executed in this system are done via smart contracts that allow automatic transferring of title or record rights to another party without the need for someone to physically verify, approve and record the rights in the registry.

A working example of this can be found in the Georgian government, where technology has been seamlessly incorporated into the existing software for land titling by making changes only in the backend.

Consequently, any input made by the citizens can be executed by blockchain by further executing a specific smart contract to carry out the necessary action.

This has helped in expediting the system, since the operation can be carried out by the citizens themselves without visiting the office. The part of the software which was being used by the citizens has been left untouched. Additionally, a strong and clean audit trail provides transparency.

Public Procurement

A major concern that citizens across the globe share is that of corruption. Most of the corruption takes place during public procurement and bidding of government orders.

The primary reason for this is that the process is often kept under wraps and manual book-keeping of these records are manipulated easily. This creates an urgency to replace the existing system with a process which is more transparent and is immune to manipulation. This is possible by incorporating a blockchain-based platform which bridges the gap between vendors and the government and also provides for enhanced accountability by concurrent oversight over operations.

A similar set up was adopted by the Colombian Inspector General's Office and the Inter-American Development Bank, wherein they created a public, permission-less Ethereum- based block chain procurement system.

The system enabled vendors and tenders to conduct the vendor bidding, while also allowing third parties such as journalists and citizens to monitor and flag risky activities in real time. The software included several automated features such as minimum bidding and automatic "red flags" to alert the Colombian Inspector General's Office regarding a potentially corrupt activity. This instance is a practical example of how technology can increase accountability, create a system of checks and balances and strengthen the fabric of democracy.

A Glimpse Into the Future

Blockchain technology holds the potential of revolutionising interactions between government, businesses and citizenry in a manner that was unimaginable before. Though often clubbed with technologies such as Internet of Things (IoT) or artificial intelligence (AI), this technology is unique in its construct.

Unlike the other technologies that have the potential of delivering entirely new services to its users, blockchain has the capacity of revamping currently existing processes and unlocking new sources of value (economy), efficiency and transparency.

Blockchain solutions enable reductions in complexity and cost of transactions while also ensuring improvement in transparency and fraud controls. The features of blockchain make it preferable in processes requiring auditability, security and decentralised access. While alternative solutions such as centralised databases with distributed API or distributed database may also solve specific issues in processes at a lower cost, blockchain has the potential of solving these challenges more seamlessly, quickly and transparently.

5.4 Crypto is the future

Cryptocurrencies are here to stay. So the government must put in place a regulatory framework to protect investors, foster innovation. The past few years have witnessed a dramatic rise in the popularity of cryptocurrencies around the world, with some touting them to be the 'digital currency of the future'. In fact, in 2018, Christine Lagarde, the Managing Director of the IMF at the time, compared its disruptive potential to the internet itself.

While such proclamations might be premature, it is important to acknowledge their growing importance and ability to reshape global finance and banking and therefore, assess its full impact and potential on the Indian digital economy.

Over the past year alone, the price of Bitcoin has multiplied more than six times, and despite its volatile nature, it is widely being viewed as an investment "asset" by businesses as well as retail investors. Its growing popularity has been powered by cryptocurrencies' main value proposition of a decentralised platform which ensures transactions with transparency and strong privacy enabled by blockchain technology. This is underlined by the overall market value of cryptocurrency exceeding $2 trillion in 2021, with estimates suggesting that seven million Indians invest and trade in crypto assets valued at over $1 billion.

The challenges

However, its exponential growth has also resulted in the focus turning to some of the perceived deficiencies in this developing technology. One major concern revolves around the volatile nature of crypto, exacerbated with the rise of 'alt coins' which critics point out can often resemble Ponzi schemes.

Cryptocurrencies are also being looked at as a source of money-laundering and its inherently decentralised nature making it far harder for authorities to regulate. Other arguments against the viability of crypto currencies point towards the security risk they entail, as well as the current lack of a solution when it comes to ensuring its effective inheritance. These are also concerns around possible asset bubbles around such currencies due to over-leveraging with possible newer types of derived products.

While these concerns and challenges do have some merit, it is natural for issues to emerge with the rise of newer technologies. This rise has also resulted in cryptocurrency networks strengthening their measures to mitigate such issues. For example, the furore around cryptocurrencies being used as a primary mode of money laundering and illicit activity has been partially negated by the integration of anti-money laundering measures such as fraud detection and flagging of suspicious transactions.

While the UN estimates 2-5 per cent of global GDP stems from illicit activities, criminal activity represented just 0.34 per cent of all cryptocurrency transactions in 2021 — a reduction from 2.1 per cent in 2019. The other major concern around price volatility and its effect on retail investors is perfectly valid, and this is where enabling regulation can play an important role in educating as well as protecting potential investors.

Right regulation

When it comes to the regulation of cryptocurrencies in India, it is important for policymakers to acknowledge the challenges discussed while simultaneously adopting a solution-based approach to any regulatory framework. Over the past few years, the Indian government's position around crypto has seen multiple shifts.

The first formal restriction on cryptocurrency transactions was put forward by the RBI in 2018. This circular prevented banks and financial institutions from enabling transactions with cryptocurrency platforms and virtual currencies. To add to this, in 2019, a Parliamentary committee formally recommended against regulating cryptocurrency and pushed for it to be banned.

However, a Supreme Court decision on this matter in 2020 gave crypto traders and investors great relief, while another encouraging sign was when Finance Minister Nirmala Sitharaman acknowledged its growing potential and the need for a "calibrated approach" towards its regulation in her Budget speech in 2022.

Despite these positive signs, there has been recent disruption in the services of cryptocurrency exchanges in India with several banks disabling payment gateways from processing transactions towards cryptocurrency platforms in the country. This recent disruption has stunted the growth of businesses, as well as created a barrier to investment opportunities for Indian consumers.

The issue is particularly relevant considering the exponential increase in the popularity of cryptocurrencies, both in terms of trading, as well as an investment asset. This factor is underlined by the overall investment in cryptocurrencies in

India increasing by 317.2 per cent over the course of 2020, according to a report by YCharts.

The growth in interest and investment in cryptocurrency has also been reflected in the rise of multiple Indian cryptocurrency trading platforms, led by the likes of WazirX and CoinDCX.

Another prominent example is Polygon, a blockchain scalability platform which helps reduce transaction time and fees across Ethereum networks and is founded by three Indians who are being billed as 'India's first crypto billionaires'. These platforms are generating foreign investment, as well as creating employment and growth opportunities for Indians.

Conclusion

It is advisable for the government to take advantage of the opportunity presented and acknowledge the important role that cryptocurrency is going to play in the future. The Centre and NITI Aayog must get into the act quickly to develop an enabling framework that involves a steady process of in-depth research and stakeholder consultation for regulation of crypto trade.

India must not waste this opportune moment to move towards a progressive form of regulation which protects consumers while ensuring optimal growth and innovation for cryptocurrencies and the ancillary industries that will emerge around it.

CHAPTER 6

ECONOMY AND DEVELOPMENT

6.1 75 years of India's Independence

India completed 75 years of being an independent nation on the 15th of August this year. Seven and a half decades into independence, India boasts of a dynamic democratic polity the foundation of which was laid down by our founding fathers eons back. The country's diversity, be it in terms of culture, language, geography, religion, ethnicity, traditions remain protected even while national integrity has become a serious challenge. Over the years, India has developed commendable international relations with world powers like United States, Russia, Japan, and European Union.

The Indian economy is also accelerating and is now being regarded to generate noteworthy global clout and force by enlarging and streamlining its military proficiency. India's aspiration to be a permanent seat at the United Nations was very well received by a lot of nations which is a testament of how India has left an imprint on the global map.

Breakdown of India's development over the years

Indian democracy has seeped through to the grass-root level via the decentralized model of governance which finds its base at Panchayati Raj establishments. This elaborate structure of governance, right from the ground percolating upwards is one of the biggest accomplishments of free India. Independent India also ensured inclusion at all levels of governance. Women have found place in several avenues including, but not limited to, police, bureaucracy, combat services, doctors, scientists, and managing directors of multi-national corporations. Affirmative action enabled by the Constitution has created opportunities for all sections of the society in education, jobs, and entrepreneurship.

The IT sector has seen a major boost over the years transforming India into a global digital player. As far as developments in space are concerned, India has successfully launched Mangalyaan (its indigenous mars obiter mission) and Chandrayaan (its very own Moon exploration mission). Beginning with a paternalistic top down beneficiary oriented Mai-Baap paradigm of development intervention, India moved to a rights based approach such as right to education (Samagra Shiksha Abhiyan Scheme), right to health (National Health Insurance Scheme, Ayushman Bharat), right to work (The National Rural Employment Guarantee Scheme) are some of the standout schemes implemented by India over the years. The India of the 21st century is a country of global vision and ambitions. It is also a crucial vaccine producer. Approximately 850 million vaccines have been dished out in India already and another 66 million vaccines to various countries around the world. India is also on its way to launch its first ever human space flight mission. The country is a global leader in advanced technologies like Cloud computing, Artificial Intelligence (AI), Internet of Things (IoT), Robotics, etc. On the energy front, India has solar and renewable sources of energy thereby ensuring sustainability.

Has India lived up to the promises made in its Preamble?

India under its Preamble declared itself a sovereign, socialist, democratic, republic securing justice, liberty, equality and fraternity to all its citizens. While the country has persevered to achieve the attributes laid down in its Constitution, there is still a long way to go. Liberty of thought and expression is a given in the Constitution, but in reality India has been slipping places in the Human Freedom Index that ranks close to 162 countries on their freedom quotient. This downgrade is mostly attributed to reasons like prolonged Internet shutdowns, subduing protests, misuse of sedition law, growing intolerance among religious groups, discriminate legislations like the Citizenship amendment, UAPA, etc. Additionally, there is also a drop in India's position on the World Press Freedom Index 2021 where it now ranks 142 among 180 nations. These international report cards are alarming. In its Preamble, India promises to all its citizens 'Justice- social, economic, and political.' However, Indian society is still infiltrated with social divisions like rich-poor, Hindu-Muslim, upper caste-lower caste, etc. Dalit killings, growing hate speech and discrimination against minorities and caste biases show that social parity is still a distant dream even after all these years of independence. There is still a huge gap in income equality in the country and the purchasing power of the poor is on the downrise. In terms of poverty, since the Consumption Expenditure Survey (CES) data hasn't been released since 2011-12, basing reliance on the Periodic Labour Force Survey, data depicts an increase in the absolute number of the poor in the country due to deterioration of the employment structure. Due to recession infused by the pandemic, India is back to being 'a country of mass poverty' after 45 years as per Pew Research Centre, using World Bank data. Employment growth has also taken a blow. The MNREGA scheme is no more able to cater to the needs of the rural poor. Economic growth in the last decade has also been meagre and the COVID situation in the country has made matters worse. This stagnancy has impacted the rural areas disproportionately. The pandemic also severely affected the rural poor in terms of online education due to lack of online resources. Independence of the judiciary has also been questioned on grounds of its allegiance being influenced by communal, political and other arbitrary biases.

Conclusion

Post independence, India has proved to be a bridge between the various extremities of the world by trying its best to live up to the basic tenets of its Constitution like secularism, democracy, law and justice, human rights, scientific temper and open and broad thinking. India has also been the flag-bearer of decolonizing movements around the world specially independence movements in Africa and Asia. While we have come so far, there is still a long way to go to achieve the status of a 'developed' country as against the current 'developing' We need to ensure that the country upholds the promise of its preamble in its true sense. We have to address inequality in power arising out of wealth, education, social status, political power and variance in employment opportunities. As a nation we need to identify problematic areas and address those issues so as to stay steadfast on our agendas and live up to the expectations of our forefathers to build an inclusive India and thereby a better future for humanity.

6.2 Does budget FY22 have federal and citizen equity?

Budget FY22 was presented at a difficult juncture not just for the Indian economy, but for the global economy. The Union Finance Minister has been bold to breach the FRBM-mandated fiscal deficit targets to stimulate growth, largely by giving a strong infrastructure boost (increase in budgeted capital investment by 34%, besides cess-funded agriculture infrastructure).

Admittedly, it is a budget that lifted the pall of gloom that had settled all around. It has set a definite and stable policy direction in the medium and long term for the country's finances and economy for attracting much-needed domestic and foreign private investment. However, a great part of responsibility of ensuring equity, both federal and citizen, is not addressed in the budget.

Federal equity

The 15th Finance Commission (FC) has recommended a reduction of 1% in the states' share of the divisible pool, to 41%, from the 42% of 14th FC, to account for the expenses for the new UTs of Ladakh and J&K, thus imposing the burden of formation of the new UTs on the states, even though it should have been borne out of the Centre's resources. Besides, a separate, non-lapsable fund of Rs 7,000 crore recommended to be carved out of the divisible pool for security and defence of the country, instead of meeting it from the central share, has depleted the divisible pool further.

The introduction of cess on petrol and diesel and the agriculture cess further makes the sharing more iniquitous as these revenues are not shareable with the states. Cess and surcharges, which were Rs 23,000 crore in FY10, have increased tenfold, to Rs 2.32 lakh crore in FY20—11.1% in 2010 to 15.6% in 2020. In addition, in Budget FY22, the cess and surcharges on 17 commodities will be roughly around Rs 70,000 crore. Hence, total cess and surcharges are pegged at more than Rs 3 lakh crore. This is equivalent to 45% of the aggregate shared taxes. Therefore, after re-adjustment of cess and non-shareable excise, the divisible pool has been effectively reduced to 30%. The 41% recommended by the 15th FC is now a delusion. The numbers in the Budget for FY22 confirm this. The Centre has pegged tax revenue at Rs 22.17 lakh crore in the Budget. Based on that, it has pegged the share of the states at Rs 6.65 lakh crore. This puts the states' share at a little more than 29%. The vertical devolution, which aims at correcting imbalances between the Centre and the states, is grossly failing to address it over time. If we look at the data, the total devolution to the states, as a percentage of Gross Tax Revenue (GTR), has declined from 32.36% in FY21BE to 30.02% in FY22BE.

The 15th FC recommends devolution based on need and equity on the one hand, and efficiency & performance on the other. However, the data says that the top five states that suffer most from devolution are mainly the low-income states, such as Uttar Pradesh, Bihar, Madhya Pradesh, and West Bengal, in the range of Rs 21,216 crore to Rs 8,892 crore. These low-income states are socially backward and have a higher need-based expenditure requirement.

Going forward, the states will have no option but to bridge the revenue shortfall through higher borrowings, affecting states' financial management owing to higher debt servicing burden (interest payments). As per the February 9, 2021, auction, the spread between the 10-year SDL and 10-year government security was 100 bps, up from the previous auction's 72 bps (February 2, 202) and 64 bps (January 25, 2021). The recent spike in yield of state governments' bond is going to increase the interest burden.

The budget provides for an enhanced outlay of Rs 1,18,101 crore for the ministry of road transport and highways, of which Rs 1,08,230 crore is for capital expenditure, the highest ever. While economic corridors in the states of Tamil Nadu, Kerala, Assam, and West Bengal have been provided for, other potential states have been completely neglected. Similar discrimination exists in railway infrastructure too.

Citizen Equity Employment

The MGNREGS has seen a 34 per cent reduction between FY21RE and FY22BE, down from Rs 1,11, 500 crore to Rs 73,000 crore. The total number of person-days of employment will reduce 17.64 per cent to 2.7-2.8 billion from 3.4 billion. The Centre has not introduced any urban employment initiatives on the lines for the MGNREGS even though states such as Odisha, Himachal Pradesh, Jharkhand, and Kerala are implementing them. The Union ministry of labour and employment, in FY22, has been allocated an amount that is 3% lower than the FY21RE. The reduction in funds to some of the schemes meant for giving wage employment is disconcerting. Major schemes that have seen a curtailment in their outlay include Bima Yojana for Unorganised Workers, Employees Pension Scheme, Pradhan Mantri Shram Yogi Maandhan, Pradhan Mantri Karam Yogi Maandhan, Pradhan Mantri Rojgar Protsahan Yojna, and National Career Services.

Agriculture and Textiles

In India, more than 65 per cent of the population is employed in agriculture and allied activities. The textiles sector is the next highest employer. But the overall outlay for agriculture has been reduced by 8 per cent and Capex in textiles by a massive 20 per cent. The allocation for PM-KISAN has also been reduced by Rs 10,000 crore, to Rs 65,000 crore from FY21BE. This is going to affect states, too, and can push millions of people into poverty. Moreover, the allocation is dismal for the two schemes that ensure the implementation of the MSP—the Market Intervention Scheme (50 per cent decrease from FY20) and PM Aannadata Aay Sanrakshan Yojana (73 per cent decrease from FY20)—as also almost all the handloom and khadi schemes and programmes. All this can negatively affect the farmers' and weavers' incomes, leading to their further impoverishment compared to the pre-Covid period. To conclude, the distorting of the fiscal federal structure, sidelining of agriculture and textile sector and neglecting unemployment issue make Budget FY22 potentially highly iniquitous.

6.3 Can Capital Expenditure boost the economy?

The debate around the ability of capital expenditure to boost long-term growth within the Indian economy, given both the pre- and the post-pandemic weak economic environment, has seen a wide range of varying opinions being presented by economists and policymakers. The Union Budget and the argument for capex: The budgetary allocation towards capital expenditure at Rs 5,54,236 crore in FY2021-22(BE) is a rise of 34.5% over FY2020-21. This is significant if we compare 21.71% rise in FY2020-21(BE) over FY2019-20(BE). This move is significant against the backdrop of the economic slowdown caused due to the Covid-19 pandemic, coupled with a decline in employment ratio.

A lack of capital expenditure has often been criticised as neglecting long-term targets of economic growth and employment. While creating direct consumer demand is an important lever for immediate boost to the economy, it may not sustain a high growth trajectory in the longer term. The creation of capital assets generates future cash flows for the economy and adds to value creation. Capital expenditure is expected to achieve this through a multiplier effect (a change in rupee value of output with respect to a change in rupee value of expenditure). In India, the multiplier effect of capital expenditure made by the central government is estimated at 2.45, whereas for state governments it is around 2 (according to the RBI Bulletin, December 2020). A Rs 1 crore increase in capital expenditure leads to more than Rs 1 crore increase in GDP. This multiplier effect works through expansion of ancillary industries and services and job creation. On the supply side also, it can facilitate labour productivity. Thus, capital expenditure is an effective tool for countercyclical fiscal policy and acts as a macroeconomic stabiliser.

Concerns

However, this multiplier effect will not take into account the time-lag to kick in, capacity availability in the industry, and undisposed inventory and work in progress before the pandemic-induced lockdowns. Most importantly, given the pandemic, the multiplier effect loses value if people hold idle cash out of fear of unforeseen expenses and survival paramountcy during possible future lockdowns. This appeared as a distinct possibility in the raging second wave of the pandemic. Inflation-induced price rise, particularly in food and health, could also affect the multiplier impact as households would tend to give them priority over other consumption items. This was indeed the case until April, 2021. Also, capital expenditure funded by the government through heavy domestic borrowing (of the order of Rs 18 lakh crore by the Centre plus Rs 78,000 crore by 21 states towards loss in GST compensation due to the lockdown effect) has the potential of crowding out capital expenditure by the private sector, thus severely weakening the multiplier effect.

Besides, for viability of a particular capital project, the Internal Rate of Return (IRR) should be more than the Hurdle Rate (HR)/Cost of Funding (CoF). The IRR depends on net cash flow generation from a capital project during its life time. The HR/CoF is decided by the cost of raising capital for the implementation of a project. The IRR should be more than the HR/CoF in order to make the project both economically and financially viable, and contribute to actual value creation in the economy. The IRR has been benchmarked for capital projects funded by the private sector. For example, the IRR on infrastructural projects on a global scale ranges between 8% and 12%. However, trends in India reveal that the range is 6-8% only, which can be a deterrent to private sector funding of infrastructural projects. Low IRR in the Indian context has traditionally been a result of cost and time overruns. According to the Ministry of Statistics and Programme Implementation (MoSPI) project database as of January 2018, 345 projects have incurred a cost overrun of Rs 2.19 lakh crore and 354 projects have time overrun of 45 months. The reasons behind these overruns are lack of forward-planning, identification of risk factors and poor collaboration amongst stakeholders. Besides, the regulatory uncertainty arising out of sudden legal, legislative changes or change in government policies like the imposition of the retrospective tax (like Vodafone and Cairn India cases) adversely impacts IRR margins. The Asian Development Bank also noted that the project implementation costs in India's transport industry were substantially higher than in Sri Lanka and China. Also, an aspect that goes under the radar is the defective and often-manipulated Detailed Project Reports (DPRs) that exaggerate output and outcome forecasts; for example, in an *ayacut* area (area served by an irrigation project such as a canal, dam or a tank) that would be irrigated once a mega or medium irrigation project is being evaluated for implementation, just to show economic viability for the project knowing fully well that, eventually, the IRR would be far less than the HR/CoF. What is also equally important is the long-term quality of capital creation, as poor quality necessitates recurring maintenance costs attached to a project after its completion.

The way forward

With the impetus rightly being given to capital expenditure, emphasis must also be provided on timely implementation of projects within the earmarked outlay by strengthening monitoring, redressal mechanisms and processes for controlling project delays. The solution lies in optimising project management processes of all the key stakeholders, including implementation agencies, state governments, vendors and others. This would also help in ensuring quality control, which, in turn, will result in capital assets providing benefits over a longer term following the multiplier effect. The maintenance, repair and operation (MRO) expenditure, which is part of revenue expenditure, will have to be monitored during project implementation to see to it that it goes on to increase the ability of the capital asset to deliver the projected benefits during the lifetime of the asset. The government should also aim to cut down on inefficient revenue expenditure and focus on creating a balanced and stable virtuous cycle, which can have positive knock-on effects over the long term. This will help set the foundation for stimulating growth and future investments, while eventually leading the economy to overcome the recessionary pressures it might once again confront if we are hit by the future waves.

6.4 MSMEs suffering due to risk averse banks

Rejecting loan applications of credit-worthy MSMEs will hurt financial inclusion and economic growth.

The Prime Minister's dream of a $5-trillion Indian economy by 2025 along with effective financial inclusion and sustainable economic outcomes is premised on investment from both domestic and foreign investors. Government expenditure can only provide a stimulus, but cannot take India to PM's goal alone.

For domestic private investments to happen, the role of timely, adequate and quality (low cost) credit cannot be overstated, particularly during the current times when Covid induced stress is maximum on almost all industries. With the recent change in the definition, more than 95 per cent of Indian companies are bought under the definition of MSMEs.

So what ails the MSME sector largely reflects the credit eco-system for more or less the entire industry in this country. The large corporate and top business houses have had any difficulty in accessing credit.

Access to Credit

Most of the MSMEs are in rural and semi-urban areas where access to credit is extremely limited. They are vulnerable to predatory moneylenders and often fall into a cycle of debt. Lack of access to finance and timely credit support in business has been a long-standing issue for these MSMEs.

Starting from difficulties faced in seeking loans and working capital from banks to delay in receiving government payments and tax refunds, most of the MSMEs are under severe debt.

As per an IFC study, there is an overall debt demand of 69.3 trillion of which 84 per cent is financed by informal sources such as moneylenders, family, friends, chit funds. Formal sources such as commercial banks, NBFCs and government institutions cater to a mere 16 per cent.

Out of these ₹10.9 trillion, ₹8.8 trillion is supplied by commercial banks while ₹1.5 trillion by NBFCs. The failure of traditional lending mechanisms to guide credit towards these MSMEs has led to a scenario where financing is often not reliable, and steady.

This has been particularly exacerbated by the pandemic, as well as the poor state of micro financing in the country, highlighted by India's estimated credit gap of over $330 billion.

Further, when more than 80 per cent of these MSMEs are in the micro and small category and depending on informal sources of credit, the usefulness of the government's emergency line credit, stressed asset relief, equity participation and fund of funds operation make very little meaning and contribution to the sector.

Banks employ various methods to limit risk by better assessment of the creditworthiness of individuals or firms, MSMEs included. To keep NPAs down, many credit worthy individuals are denied loans by banks.

While determining creditworthiness, there are two errors that are common—False Acceptance of a bad applicant and False Rejection of a good applicant. The former error is detrimental for banks and increases risk while the latter impacts financial inclusion and economic growth itself.

Many MSMEs have an existing barrier in terms of accessing credit. A false rejection of a good applicant paired with the existing structural issues relating to access to credit for this sector exacerbates the issue. While there is plethora of punitive actions prescribed against commissions of irregular loan financing, there is complete absence of punitive action against omissions of genuine credit financing of businesses, particularly the MSMEs.

Thus, there is no incentive for bank managers to take risks

and finance genuine credit requirements.

This kind of approach to credit adversely impacts both growth and financial inclusion. However, the government sought a list of investment-grade companies denied emergency credit by banks in the backdrop of the Covid pandemic though what action the government took on the recalcitrant banks remains unknown.

Banks will have to move away from financing collateral to financing the business or the business plans.

Another issue is the lack of paperwork or digital footprint for small MSMEs, a factor which holds them back from being integrated into the formal economy and deprives the MSMEs to take advantage of the formal credit system.

They continue to gain access to credit against assets such as land, etc. when much of the MSME development has started to follow a digital model.

Recording transactional details such as utility payments, electricity bills, etc. would give insight into the financial behaviour of these entities that can aid in extending credit coverage to the unserved/underserved MSMEs.

The way forward

Focused regulatory and structural changes which will improve access, ease the transition to the formal sector and increase consumer education and protection are necessary.

In the long term, once these regulatory issues are addressed, sanctioned loans will be disbursed more easily and private investment will be boosted, creating a virtuous cycle for MSMEs in the country.

Finally, to minimise the false rejections of good applicants, routine audits of all loan applications on random sampling basis must be undertaken by RBI and administrative action taken against malafide omissions resulting in unethical denial of loans to deserving MSMEs.

6.5 MSMEs need the right push: Atmanirbharta needs to address historical barriers

The MSME sector contributes approximately 40% to the GDP and generates employment for 114 million Indians, comprising about 93% of the total labour force of the country. However, over the last few years, economic distress has plagued the sector on several counts, and this has only exacerbated by the current pandemic. All India Manufacturers Organisation (AIMO) suggests that 35% MSME businesses are now beyond recovery. The sector is, thus, staring at massive unemployment, only to worsen the unemployment problem, which was already at a 45-year high prior to the shutdowns and the lockdowns.

The government's commitment to revive the MSME sector was revealed in its Rs 20,000 crore economic stimulus package for Atmanirbhar India, which includes a Rs 10,000 crore fund to finance equity infusion. However, credit guarantee has a limited appeal as only 15% of the credit requirement is fulfilled through formal financial channels; 86% of the enterprises are unregistered, and 71% of the workers have no contracts, therefore, opening new lines of credit may not be adequate to revive the sector. The Finance Minister indicated that the sanctioned loans are not being availed and utilised by enterprises in the absence of strong demand and consumption.

The UK Sinha-led expert committee on MSME in 2019 highlighted the need to create an enabling environment for

MSMEs. It proposed several long-term solutions to ensure financial sustainability. However, a holistic MSME policy rests on the ability to overcome some historical barriers.

First, the inability to receive timely payments in return for the goods and services, and slim profit margins is a nagging issue. An urgent solution is the payment of dues. More loans—a supply-side solution—cannot resolve the limited working capital problem as it would unnecessarily increase the debt burden, which, in turn, would put pressure on the already thin margins. A new regime, based on discounting for early clearance of dues by their principals or all supplies being made against advance payments or creating a hold in the bank which gets released right after receipt of supply from the MSME supplier, could be alternatives. Only an incentive-based mechanism will work. Second, the average cost of capital is still high, at around 13%, compared to agriculture. It is challenging to generate an IRR over 13% in the near future to pay back loans availed at almost the same rate or even higher, and even if they could, the gestation period for demand to pick up will continue for 5-6 years. To help MSMEs avail capital at sub-5% rates, lending institutions must reduce transaction costs.

Third, historically, a lack of internal competitiveness in the industry has reduced the urgency for innovation within the sector, despite the 'Make in India' and 'Startup India' campaigns. This requires support to reorient production lines and investments in R&D.

Last, the sector has been unable to channelise a global market for products and services. The current crisis has drastically contracted export-led growth opportunities as importing nations adopt a protectionist policy. With the global demand at an all-time low, consumers are not compelled to make non-essential purchases. A lot of our exports such as textiles, perfumes, jewellery and gems are non-essential goods and services which would see negative pressures after Covid and lockdown, including the IT and IT-enabled export market. Only 3% of MSME respondents in the AIMO survey suggest that they will be unaffected as the business is focused on essential goods. A sustained push through e-commerce channels can enhance the scope of domestic goods and services with low transaction and intermediation cost. It will also help eliminate the middleman and reduce cost of doing business, an important factor in the survival of small businesses.

India has the opportunity to leverage its technological prowess in enhancing the competitive advantage that we already have in the export of IT/ITes products and services. The rise of AI, IT, digital learning and communication-based businesses are evolving the traditional business paradigm, and MSME's should be encouraged to harness this through the right kind of policy push. The government must adopt a comprehensive approach to revamp the MSME ecosystem.

6.6 India's action plan to compete with China

China will never stop bullying its neighbours. Military escalation and de-escalation across borders will continue. India needs to reduce the power asymmetry with its neighbour and build its muscles so that it can flex them from a position of strength. This asymmetry exists across four areas—economic, diplomatic, political and military. Therefore, a holistic strategy is necessary to make India stronger and help it respond more effectively to any such future threat to the country.

Economic strength

India can build economic clout through better business planning. The aversion to large-scale industries was a mistake. To make India an economic power, we need to do mass production. It will help achieve cost leadership and beat China's pricing. Around 80% of air conditioners, 70% of mobile sets, 60% of shoes, 74% of solar cells and 60% of premium luxury branded products in the world are now being manufactured in China. Will our MSMEs be able to scale up production and match China in pricing and quality in the global market? Maybe yes, but we need to build clusters for that—and a one district one product strategy where MSMEs can share technology, expertise and labour, and bring efficiency for mass production.

However, the best solution would be mass production by big companies, so that India can enjoy cost leadership in international markets and replace China as the export partner of many countries. India can identify 10,000 companies with a Rs 100 crore+ turnover, and have the vision to grow big and dominate the international market with large-scale production. The government can help them in exports and business by signing trade agreements with friendly countries through India's diplomatic and strategic initiatives.

The government needs to provide them loans at an interest rate of 3-4% to allow them to invest in technology and equipment to scale up their production.

Before that, India needs to address some ground issues, such as skilling of workers, making power available at Rs 3 per unit to industries (that's the rate in China), building wide and efficient roads, rails, ports and airports to reduce transportation costs, and changing labour laws, etc.

Diplomatic strength

This is one area where it is not understood why India should have an asymmetry in power. India needs to develop business skills in its diplomats. We need to skill and re-skill them to focus and achieve both strategic and business goals from the relations with the countries they are stationed in. With Covid-19, we have an opportunity to improve on the business partnership matrix and trade relations to achieve phenomenal business growth year on year, starting from 2021.

The 'train the trainer' program conducted for business leaders from corporates and senior diplomats with business acumen can help sharpen their business skills, which are necessary for partnership development and signing business contracts. The External Affairs Ministry needs to assess the present skill gaps and develop training programmes accordingly.

Secondly, in a world in which the US and China are more confrontational and competitive now, India needs to decide which bloc it should go with. The US has been interested in building better and stronger relationships with India as a counter balance to China, particularly in the Asian continent.

Now, the FVEY countries, (the Five eyes Alliance—the US, UK, Australia, New Zealand and Canada) are reorienting their policies towards China as a consequence of the pandemic and looking towards India to play a dominant role in the Indo-Pacific region. It is India that needs to respond to these global calls and take proactive measures to converge politically, strategically and economically with every country for its own benefits. And relationships with our immediate neighbours are important to maintain peace in the region. Then, we need to create a task force of MPs across political parties to engage various countries for trade and business partnerships—setting clear goals to achieve business/trade revenue growth—and aligning them to this goal of making India a super economic power.

When they visit another country, they can take 10 Indian businessmen along with them, so they can explore business opportunities and sign deals there.

Political strength

Democracy continues to remain our strength as it gives us a leverage in our engagements with other larger and more powerful democracies of the world as they celebrate individual choice and freedom unlike communist China. While there are counter arguments to the above assertion citing delayed decision-making due to time wasted in arriving at a consensus or a majority, it has been proved that democracies are able to deliver citizens their rights much better than a communist set-up. We need to strengthen our democracy by making it more mature, erudite and less raucous.

Military strength

India needs to get into strategic partnerships with advanced defence powers like the US, Russia, France, the UK, Israel, Japan, and most of the China-wary countries in the Indo-Pacific region such as South Korea, Vietnam, Australia, New Zealand, Indonesia, Taiwan and the Philippines. Then we need to build our indigenous capabilities and military competence with investments in defence technologies and production. For that, we need to increase our defence budget manifold. This is the time for India to have a solid long-term strategic plan to grow stronger—economically, technologically, militarily and politically—without being overly aggressive in challenging China over a longer period of time and a larger geopolitical space.

6.7 Aligning with other nations for Atmanirbhar+

Blue Ocean Strategy can give India a competitive edge and help it connect better with the rest of the world. Such an approach suggests that business firms should stop getting into cut-throat competition and price wars while selling 'me-too' products in a cluttered market. There is no point for companies to stay put in a red ocean and see all the bloodshed by different players in an existing market or segment. Instead, they should explore newer opportunities with new businesses and product ideas, thereby creating a new market segment and new demand—and probably entry barriers—so that they enjoy market dominance, mindshare and higher profitability.

Can India adopt a Blue Ocean Strategy and apply it to its Atmanirbhar policy? The idea of self-reliance is good. However, it should not be restricted to the thought of reducing India's economic dependence on China or boycotting their products. We need to take the idea to the next level and make India invincible all over the world by being price competitive and quality superior. Starting with his inaugural address in the India Global Week 2020 and even in his address to the UN General Assembly, Prime Minister Narendra Modi has emphasised that Atmanirbhar Bharat is not about looking inward and being closed and self-contained, and thus becoming uncompetitive, but about self-sustenance and self-generation and to a scale that it feeds the entire world. He said: 'We are laying a red carpet for all global companies to come and establish their presence in India. Very few countries will offer the kind of opportunities that India does today.'

This is the right time for both the Ministry of Commerce and Industry and the Ministry of External Affairs to reach out to most of the world nations hurt economically by Covid-19, believed to have been inflicted on the world by China. India can engage with them in trade and export products that they used to get from China earlier or even now. This could be achieved through a number of bilaterally or regionally negotiated Free Trade Agreements (FTAs). However, this strategy will work only if our products and services are price competitive and superior in quality to the same or similar products or services that they used to import from China. We would therefore need to expand and alter the composition of our export basket.

With bulk orders in hand, Indian companies can ramp up production and command cost leadership—which China used to enjoy earlier. This is the time when India can play with the 'economies of scale'. An Atmanirbhar-plus strategy is a step forward from the above, and it's more than just being swadeshi, producing and consuming our own products, and then thinking of exports. But does it make any business sense? Why would other nations be interested in importing from us? What do we have to offer them in return?

In Atmanirbhar-plus, we will have a collaborative, partnership approach to reduce the bloodshed, enjoy market dominance and profitability in a maximum of 3,000 identified products and in other goods where we already have a surplus and have been exporting for quite some time. We need to partner with other friendly nations across the globe, both big and small, especially with Russia, Burma, Bangladesh, Sri Lanka, Taiwan, Japan, Indonesia, Vietnam, Malaysia, Philippines from our own Asian region—so as to build a collaborative platform to manufacture or produce in scale and then export to meet the world's demand and reduce their dependence on China.

In such a production-cum-export partnership arrangement that may go beyond the bilateral to regional arrangements, the countries need to agree that they won't clutter the world market and get into price wars by coming up with 'me-too' products. Instead, every country can leverage its natural resources, skill-sets and strengths and produce unique or agreed products. And every participating and partnering country can enjoy cost leadership because of bulk production.

This arrangement may not be possible for all the product categories. But it's a workable solution for ones where countries do not have resources, infrastructure or expertise—and they can agree not to manufacture such goods and increase the cost of production. With a pre-meditated partnership approach, we will be able to create a win-win situation for every partner so that each nation benefits from the arrangement.

If we can successfully implement such an Atmanirbhar-plus strategy by partnering with at least 100+ countries, there would be an influx of overseas orders as well as foreign investments, helping create more jobs. We can make the partner countries agree and sign the above production-cum-export partnership treaty or trade agreements, which should remain valid for at least 10 years, after which any nation would be free to review the arrangement and see if it's helping them. The US made the mistake of outsourcing manufacturing to just one country, and then a bigger mistake by not reviewing the strategy even once in three decades. The new world order and our own national leadership can learn from this.

Atmanirbhar-plus will create more economic opportunities. If implemented efficiently, it can help bring the economy back on track, with large-scale production and bulk exports, and create jobs. This will put more money in the hands of people, spur demand, incentivise production, increase investment in technology, expand the economy, help modernise the military and build up a nuclear arsenal and more. All of these would happen only if we forge a business partnership with other friendly nations.

6.8 Single window clearance not enough to solve licensing problems

An interaction with global Indian entrepreneurs showed that the seamless, scalable, process re-engineered and technologically-advanced online single window government clearance/licensing system, that the government boasts of, is still not able to lure *pravasi* Indians to invest in their country of origin. They compare the Indian licensing regime with other parts of the world — where it is free from red-tapism and other bureaucratic inconsistencies at the ground level.

Too many licences

A San Francisco-based Indian-origin entrepreneur wondered why he needs to apply for 50 different licences to produce an Ayurveda medicine. He would need separate licences for industry, factory, boilers, electricity supply, generators, pollution, labour, fire, water, alcohol, drugs, Ayush, laboratory, excise, GST, sales, import, export etc. In addition, he must get some licences from the State government and some from the Central government. Obtaining dozens of clearances from multiple authorities, even in a single-window, is a herculean task, because one needs to do a lot of paperwork. Most of the times, what is explained in the policies and mentioned on websites is not followed by the authorities themselves. If the above-mentioned entrepreneur would like to do his business in the US, he may need just a quick approval from the FDA and two more licences — one each from the state and the federal governments. Before selling anything, he just needs to prove that his products are safe and stable for consumers by running what are called stability tests as prescribed under good manufacturing practices set by the FDA. Can't we replicate this in India? Can't we just allow such companies to do stability tests on their finished products and get rid of the various licences required before the plant is even set up? If not, is there a possibility where the Parliament can pass a law to reduce these existing 50 or so licences to just 10, with an agreement or a non-repudiatory contract covering the remaining requirements, that the entrepreneur can read and sign? If one wants to get into a restaurant business in Singapore or China, all they need is just four licences, whereas here it is 12-16 licences, depending on the State. The number is greater in metro cities — 26 in Delhi and Bengaluru and 22 in Mumbai. Plus, there is a 'police eating house licence' required in Delhi and Kolkata. And, the number of documents needed to obtain this licence from the Delhi Police is 45. Do we need these many documents to be read, signed and submitted for approval?

Too many licensing authorities

If one wants to get into a small spice business in our country, one needs to get a trade licence from the local municipal authority, followed by Udyog Aadhar, MSME registration and many more for availing subsidies under various schemes of the government. Then, there is food business licence/FSSAI licence, BIS certification, Agmark Certification, IEC, and compliance with all the FPO regulations.

In the US, the FDA regulates drugs, medical devices, clinical research, healthcare delivery, food safety, food packaging, nutrition and everything else related to drug, food and health. In India, why do we need so many licences and certifications from the FSSAI, BIS, Agmark etc.? Can't we create a single organisation that addresses all approvals, licences, certifications, etc in one go?

Export nightmare

The nightmare actually begins when an entrepreneur starts sending shipment to outside India. A shipment that costs $2 to ship from Taiwan, Philippines, Singapore or Vietnam to the US, goes up to $10 to ship from India to the US. Then, the shipment goes through 50 inspections before it is given clearance from the port, adding to the transaction costs for the entrepreneur. Most times, the business owner needs to bribe the officers to get the shipment through. If the process of manufacturing and then exporting to global markets is so torturous, how can we expect global Indians to come back and set up businesses in India?

Pollution control headaches

Most entrepreneurs perpetually complain about handling the State pollution control boards and Ground Water Authority (CGWA) officials. They say that even if one ensures cent per cent effluent treatment and more rainwater harvesting than groundwater extracted, it is still difficult to handle the officials of these two departments. So, can we reorganise the National Green Tribunal (NGT) and bring pollution control boards and CGWA under it, in order to bring efficiency and remove corruption? Maybe, a legislation in this regard is needed.

Why is 'Make in India' not able to achieve its goals? The contribution from manufacturing to GDP was even less after a year of the 'Make in India' campaign. Why is there a dip in private investment in the last three years, despite substantial improvement in ease of doing business rankings? It is because we are not able to see and analyse things that are not working at the micro level. We are missing the fine prints for the big banners. This is the time to bring new legislation and change old laws to reduce paperwork and expedite processing.

6.9 Fighting Corruption

Odisha Chief Minister Naveen Patnaik took everyone by surprise in 2020 when he declared that all State government officials and functionaries of the Biju Janata Dal, including himself, would henceforth be mandatorily required to file their property returns with the Lok Ayukta at the end of every year. Further, all these returns would be disclosed publicly on a web portal.

This may well be the first attempt to hit out at the politico-bureaucratic nexus that has largely been attributed to the growing systematic, grassroots corruption in India. While detecting and punishing the corrupt, if caught, always remained in the rule book, the preventive aspect remained neglected.

Though the Lokpal and Lok Ayuktas Act, 2013 has existed for more than half a decade nationally, its implementation has been patchy. The deadline to file the property declarations has been constantly deferred. Initially set at September 15, 2014, it has been extended six times.

Reducing info asymmetry

Public declaration of assets of all political and bureaucratic functionaries from the panchayat to the party president level makes sense because this fundamentally seeks to promote transparency between the citizens and those in power at every level by reducing the information asymmetry.

Information asymmetry is the primary culprit for the infamous principal-agent problem that breeds rent seeking behaviour and creation of ill-gotten wealth by the agents (in this case bureaucrats and political functionaries) acting on behalf of the actual principals who are the ordinary citizens.

What makes the Odisha declaration more relevant is the possibility of creating evidence to fight corruption — a baseline data-base of assets that can provide significant insights into the asset ownership pattern of officials at different positions and portfolios in the government and which can be extrapolated to identify 'outliers' for further surveillance and investigation.

Increasing accountability

In one of the most widely used frameworks to understand systemic corruption, American academic Robert Klitgaard argues that 'corruption (C) depends on monopoly (M), discretion (D), and accountability (A),' often denoted as C = M + D – A. However, drawing from my experience as a bureaucrat, I believe that people's participation (P) is critical in preventing, detecting and, therefore, reducing corruption in the system. I, therefore, read the formula as C = M + D – A – P. More the participation by people, less is the likelihood of corruption. People's participation can increase if more information about assets of agents/seats of power is published regularly.

The Odisha declaration does this and more. For, the State government has also adopted technology in a big way and online transactions to reduce discretion. Accountability has also been addressed through tough action taken against recalcitrant government servants. In 2020 alone, about 100 government servants have been dismissed, removed or compulsorily retired.

More can be done

Admittedly, this will not be the end of the fight against corruption.

While it is a good preventive step, it is not only the severity of the punishment but the certainty of detection that would deter the corrupt. Once the new preventive mechanism kicks in, processes to monitor irregularities and outliers will need to be developed by Lok Ayuktas.

Current monitoring practices rely only on inspections and raids, mostly on intelligence reports. However, we need to move towards an institutional approach in identifying targets of those inspections. Randomised audits using technology and artificial intelligence without any human bias in selection of the auditee (in this case those who file the returns), can be the next logical step.

Protecting whistleblowers

One other key element in ensuring the effectiveness of this anti-corruption exercise will be promoting and safeguarding whistle-blowers. Although the Whistle Blower Protection Act, 2014 was passed at the Central level, the law itself is not operational yet.

Since those who enjoy power may try to find ways around the new requirement through family or proxies, who should be subject to the Prohibition of Benami Property Transactions Act, 1988 by the Income-Tax Department, it is important that the Odisha Lok Ayukta nurtures a safe environment for whistle-blowers by maintaining their anonymity besides other measures. Odisha can show the way to the country in this respect too by notifying a separate framework for protection of whistle-blowers.

Corruption has a huge economic cost. The UN estimates that developing countries lose approximately $1.26 trillion to corruption, bribery, theft and tax evasion, every year. Moreover, governments risk losing the trust of the citizens if their officials and their political masters are not held accountable for wrongdoing.

However, knowledge of officials' assets among the people, complemented with protection for whistle-blowers and certainty of punishment can create an environment that can be conducive towards cleaner and efficient governance regime.

6.10 Bring cess, surcharge in divisible pool—State Revenue

Recently, the Odisha chief minister pleaded with the Government of India for a share of the cess and surcharge collected by the Centre. This issue has also been raised in Parliament from time to time. As a part of division of power and responsibilities between the Union and states as prescribed in the Seventh Schedule under Article 246 of the Constitution, the Centre is empowered to levy and collect both direct and indirect taxes under the Union List. This, ab initio, has created a huge imbalance in resource mobilisation to the detriment of the states for meeting their committed social expenditure responsibilities.

As per the XV Finance Commission, states bear more than 62% of expenditure responsibilities but are given only 37% of revenue raising power, while the Union government owns 63% of revenue raising power to spend on 38% of its expenditure responsibilities. The Finance Commission, which is constituted under Article 280 of the Constitution to mitigate this imbalance, is assigned the responsibility of recommending the quantum of transfer of these taxes (net) to the states every five years, following objective and rational criteria in the best traditions of cooperative federalism. Such resource transfer is a 'basic feature' of the federal structure. The net proceeds of taxes (called, net tax revenue) are obtained by excluding cesses and surcharges, cost of collection and transfer to the National Disaster Response Fund (NDRF) from the gross figures of tax revenue. Therefore, a higher pool size of cesses and surcharges diminishes the overall size of the divisible tax cake, thereby adversely affecting resource transfer to the states.

The constitutional scheme

A cess, imposed on the base tax liability of a corporation or individual taxpayer, is imposed for a specific purpose. A surcharge is a tax on tax and is imposed on the people covered in the tax base only. It can be used for any public purpose as decided by the Union government. Both the proceeds are not shared with the states, this being an exception under Article 270 of the Constitution.

Impact on shareable pool

Over the years, the Union government has made use of cesses and surcharges an additional revenue mobilisation measure. Their share as percentage of gross tax revenue has more than doubled, from 6.26% in 2010-11 to 16.89% in 2021-22 (Budget Estimate). From 2010-11 to 2013-14, the Centre imposed 15 cesses and surcharges, which peaked to 25 in 2019-20. The introduction of GST has, however, subsumed many of these. During 2020-21 and 2021-22, nine were in operation. However, the levy on account of these nine cesses and surcharges was very high at Rs 3,72,971 crore during the years 2020-21 and 2021-22 as compared to average levy of Rs 1,10,180 crore during the years 2010-11 to 2019-20. This was mainly because of an increase in effective rate of road and infrastructure cess as additional duty of excise on motor spirit and high speed diesel oil. In 2018-19, Rs 51,266 crore was collected from this cess, which increased to Rs 2,24,000 crore in 2020-21. This cess was collected for the particular purpose of development and maintenance of roads. Despite increase in cesses and surcharges from Rs 49,628.02 crore in 2010-11 to Rs 3,74,471.14 crore in 2021-22, the benefits do not flow down to the states as these are not included in the divisible pool, which is net of taxes. As a result, the total divisible pool is itself declining over the years as a percentage of gross tax revenue. Although a higher devolution to states was recommended by the XIV Finance Commission (2015-2020) from 32% to 42%, the actual devolution to states (as % of gross tax revenue) remained at 34% during the said period. Similarly, the XV Finance Commission (2021-2026) recommended devolution to states at 41%. However, again in FY 2020-21 (B.E), the devolution to states (vertical transfers) had actually declined to 30% of gross tax revenue due to the cesses and surcharges in the total collection. If the entire cesses and surcharges projected in BE of 2021-22 were shared with the states as a part of the divisible pool in the same formula as prescribed by the XV Finance Commission, then the states would have gotten an additional kitty of Rs 1,53,533 crore (41% of Rs 3,74,471 crore).

State's demands

Over the years, states have been continuously demanding that the Union government either completely do away with cesses or if they are continued for a longer period, bring them into the divisible pool. By this inclusion, states will get a greater share of devolution from the Centre's net proceeds in order to meet their own social, human development and infrastructure commitments. Further, the Comptroller and Auditor General of India has raised serious concerns over misutilisation of cesses with only a part being spent for the particular purpose for which they were levied; the rest were diverted for other purposes. The fourteenth and fifteenth Finance Commission had recommended that revenues from cesses and surcharges should be a part of the divisible pool, by bringing about a constitutional amendment.

Conclusion

During the pandemic, it is the states that were at the forefront of testing, tracing and treatment protocol from end to end.

States were running out of resources and were heading for a fiscal crisis. The average tax to GSDP ratio of all states declined to 5.8% in 2020-21 from 6.3% in 2019-20. Besides, the average interest burden ratio for all states, measured by interest payment as percentage of revenue receipts, increased to 14.8% in 2020-21 from 12.7% in 2019-20. As a result, the average revenue deficit ratio for all states worsened to (-) 2.9% in 2020-21 from (-) 0.08% in 2019-20. Since the states are constrained to generate new resources, it is imperative that the Centre brings in a constitutional amendment to bring cesses and surcharges to the divisible pool. The Covid crisis provides the perfect backdrop for moving ahead.

6.11 Power sector amendments propose more government control

The Ministry of Power (MoP) published draft amendments to the Electricity Act, 2003, on April 17, 2020. Power is in the Concurrent List and administered both by the central and state governments. In the draft amendment Bill 2020, MoP, inter alia, proposed setting up of Electricity Contract Enforcement Authority (ECEA), which will have jurisdiction to adjudicate upon matters regarding specific performance of contracts even while retaining State Electricity Regulatory Commissions (SERCs) set up under the earlier Electricity Act, 2003. There are also several other changes proposed.

Questionable intent

Firstly, MoP has proposed certain amendments to Section 86(1)(f) of the 2003 Act to avoid any conflict with the newly incorporated Section 109A which talks about ECEA. The original Section 86(1)(f) of the 2003 Act entrusted the power of adjudication of disputes between the licensee and generating companies to state commissions, who could refer them to arbitration, if necessary. The Supreme Court, in GUVNL v Essar Power, had held that all disputes, and not merely those pertaining to matters referred to in clauses (a) to (e) and (g) to (k) in Section 86(1), between the licensee and generating companies can be resolved by state commissions or an arbitrator appointed by it. Post amendment, this position will get altered and the powers of state commissions in dispute resolution will be enjoyed by ECEA.

Secondly, the amendment proposes to make it mandatory for ERCs to reduce cross-subsidy in the manner as will be provided in the tariff policy to be announced by the Centre from time to time (as per Section 3 of the parent legislation), by withdrawing this power from SERCs who currently enjoy this power under Section 42 of the parent Act. It was up to the discretion of SERCs to order removal of such cross-subsidies. Post amendment, this power of state governments or SERCs will be scrapped. The potential consequences of such an arrangement could be problematic as tariff rates suggested by the Centre might not address state-specific challenges.

Therefore, MoP has to clearly specify the intention behind the proposed amendment and how it would succeed in achieving the objective of continuing reforms in this sector.

More government

There is also the question of the need for creating another authority when there is already ERC. Several other sectors such as telecom, civil aviation, etc, which have their own regulatory bodies, do not have such a dual authority structure. The regulators also perform the function of enforcement in these cases. The Association of Power Producers (representative body of private power generators) has raised apprehension that 'we may waste great effort and time on fight for jurisdictional space between ECEA and ERCs. For instance, on the multi-state PPAs, it took three years to get clarity from the Supreme Court. There should be a clear demarcation between the two authorities.'

Centre superseding states' rights

The Centre plays a major role in ensuring monitoring, reporting and accounting of crucial parameters in this sector. Given the varying ground-level realities and governance frameworks in states, directing more powers to the Centre would mean subversion of states' rights and possible impairment of their interests, thereby dealing a lethal blow to cooperative federalism. There will be no flexibility at the state level to alter the design and implementation to suit states' needs. Thus, changes proposed to Section 42 and 86, being in direct encroachment of state powers, must be revisited.

Other lacunae

While discoms can engage franchisees or sub-distribution licensees to distribute electricity on their behalf in a particular area under new proposals, the amendment is silent on signing of the requisite PPA between them. Absence of a legal contractual backing denudes the entire arrangement from the trust that is so essential for successful and efficient implementation of this arrangement. Such a clause was prevalent in the 2018 draft amendment Bill and needs to be reincorporated in the new draft.

Conclusion

The 37th report of the Parliamentary Standing Committee on Energy noted that the power sector had Rs 6 lakh crore of bank loans as of June 2017. Of this, Rs 37,941 crores is NPAs, while restructured advances amounted to Rs 60,858 crores. It would have been worthwhile had the proposed amendments focused more on how to deal with the prevalent losses than to bring in more complex enforcement mechanisms so as to confuse consumers.

6.12 Resuscitate the automobile sector

It is no secret that the pandemic hit the sectors that were reeling the most. A prime example is the automobile sector, which was experiencing a slowdown well before the virus hit Indian shores. The industry had been battling against a host of issues—declining consumer demand, difficulty in transitioning into BS-VI technology, extinguishing inventories of left-over BS-IV vehicles, and credit crunch in the NBFC sector. Post-lockdown, it will have to deal with a completely new environment, right from manufacturing capabilities and inventory management to emergency response mechanisms. Could the electric vehicle (EV) segment become a permanent and significant part of this new order?

Global forecasts

Today, studies from research universities claim that by 2050, every second car produced globally would be electrically powered. While marketing lessons teach us the importance of consumer acceptance for the successful adoption of any concept, research by Deloitte Global Automotive says that over 50% of the consumers are still unclear about the safety of the battery and the availability of adequate charging stations. Surprisingly, more than two-thirds of the consumers surveyed mentioned that their biggest fear is sharing the highway with heavy commercial vehicles driving in autonomous mode. Yet, what has been seen is that despite high resistance to the introduction of CNG vehicles during the mid-1990s, consumers accepted the technology widely, so much so that a few big brands now have their factory-produced MUVs and SUVs retrofitted with CNG-run engines.

Indian scenario

The EV industry in India managed to post a decent 20% increase in sales in FY20 compared to FY19. Out of the 156,000 units that the industry sold in FY20, the bulk came from the electric two-wheelers segment. The industry believes that going forward, the fastest growth would come from the e-rickshaws and e-autos segment. The fact that the President of the US was ferried to the Taj Mahal by e-vehicles has not gone unnoticed by industry players! However, the uptake of this segment has not been as rapid as expected, despite a slew of measures and incentives provided by the government. From a tax point of view, the GST council reduced the rates from 12% to 5% for vehicles, and from 18% to 5% for vehicle chargers. The Delhi 2019 e-Vehicle Policy aims at introducing more than 35,000 e-vehicles, and adding capacity of 250 charging and battery-swapping stations. It envisions the adoption of EVs such that they constitute at least 25% of all new vehicle registrations by 2024. The National Electric Mobility Mission plan 2020 (NEMP) is also aligned similarly. The Kerala government has brought in a major policy shift, instructing all its departments to purchase only e-vehicles from the next financial year.

Schemes like FAME (Faster Adoption and Manufacturing of Hybrid and Electric Vehicles) have certainly incentivised local manufacturing and the growth of domestic technology. Looking at how other countries are keen to take their manufacturing out of China and are looking for alternative destinations, it is paramount that India steps up to offer them an attractive ecosystem in this sector in the post-Covid world. As global supply chains have been disrupted due to the crisis, the requirements of lithium-ion cells will be addressed by the upcoming 40 GWH of installed Li-ion capacity plants in India, which itself is a great opportunity.

Possibilities for growth in demand

Going forward, there are a lot of growth drivers for this industry in the new normal.

Firstly, its commercial advantages should lead to a surge in the usage of e-rickshaws and e-carts in short distance logistics, and last-mile connectivity in the e-commerce segment. Second, surveys find that younger consumers, particularly females, more willing to invest in Evs than older generation. As India is overwhelmingly young, this presents a bright future for EV manufacturers.

Given that personal mobility is going to pick up again post-Covid, there should be a further policy push (beyond what has already been announced in successive budgets) for a visible shift towards increased EV adoption, particularly since consumers are seeing the benefits of a cleaner environment.

Banks should devise innovative credit schemes (now that repo rate is low) to push for such a shift. Simultaneously, the government should focus on augmenting the charging infrastructure and have in place a scrappage policy that drives new-vehicle sale. In the longer term, the existing brands will need to go for more indigenisation to make the vehicles more affordable and maintenance easier, with quick availability of parts (no dependence on import). This would ensure better services to customers; this, as of now, is a pain point. Besides, wireless and on-the-go charging are the new technologies coming up that might boost sales.

EVs are the only way to decarbonise the transport sector and achieve India's ambitious target of complete green mobility by 2030.

6.13 Dying handloom industry – Time to affect a Covid-induced disruption in policy discourse

On the eve of the National Handloom Day on 7th August, 2021 the Textile Minister Piyush Goyal called for increasing the handloom export to the tune of 10,000 crores and doubling the production in the next three years for promoting the sector. The vision was shared to uplift the pandemic stricken vulnerable handloom and handicraft sector. According to the data published by the Director General of Foreign Trade, handloom products have recorded a negative growth rate of 32% during the first quarter of 2020 vis-a-vis 2019. With sales dipping to the tune of 60-70%, it is one of the highest negative growth rates among major commodities. In the absence of adequate sales, artisans have become vulnerable and are forced to take up odd menial jobs to make ends meet. Currently, the handloom industry is operating at just 25-30% of pre-covid levels, vociferating desperate calls for help from the weaving community.

According to the Fourth All India Handloom Census (2019-20), the sector provides livelihood to 31.45 lakh weaving households, making it the second-largest source of employment in the country. Despite its cultural and economic significance, 67.1% of the total households engaged in it have a monthly income lower than Rs. 5,000. As the industry is largely reliant on exports for generation of revenue, the ongoing pandemic has worsened the already vulnerable state of affairs with irregular or no supply of yarn and dyes and collapse of marketing channels. Since the entire sector more or less operates in the informal sector, the impact has been even more severe. If the twin shocks of demonstration and GST had dealt a body blow to this sector and the weavers dependent on it, the lockdown delivered the final death knell. It is time to move fast.

Failure of conventional measures

As early as 1979, the Sivaraman Committee Report stated, 'every new powerloom made six handlooms redundant and led to large scale unemployment in the rural area.' The conclusions drawn by this committee and various others committees led to the passing of the Handloom Reservation Act, 1985 whereby 11 basic essential items were reserved to be produced only on handloom. Unfortunately, this is not strictly implemented to date. The government also introduced handloom marks in 2000, the Geographical Indicator Act in 2003 and the All India Handloom Brand in 2015 to promote handlooms, all of which have largely failed to deliver. Apart from these, recently the government abolished the All India Handloom Board and All India Handicrafts Board. Even the Budget 2021 announcement to set up textile parks in the country is more likely to benefit powerloom sector as compared to the handloom industry since handloom weavers operate out of their respective homes. Experience shows that the infrastructure model of creating common weaving centres such as ones established in Kota and Pochampalli have also failed miserably on the ground. Government's effort at registering handloom units as MSME units have also not borne much fruit since the field level functionaries who deal with them at the district level are officials of the Directorate & Textiles who have no connection with the officials of the MSME department located in the districts.

Separate policies for handloom and powerloom

The ailing handloom industry can be resuscitated only through robust disruptive interventions. The first and foremost is to treat the handloom and powerloom industry as separate entities as they are distinctly different in so far as production process, volume and marketing systems and pricing are concerned. The Ministry of Textiles makes one consolidated Textile Policy in which the policy for handlooms finds a few pages as a poor cousin. If numbers could tell a story, decline in the share of handloom cloth production over the decades makes a significant point. The share of handloom cloth production which stood at 24.98% in the year 1980-81, has continuously declined, now accounting for a meagre 15.02%. Similarly, exports of handloom products have reduced from $370 million in 2013-14 to $353 million in 2017-18. This is because the marketing of handloom products is clubbed with the overall marketing policy for textiles which largely includes powerloom products. The result is that the handloom sector has to continuously beg for government assistance to survive which is not a happy proposition.

These two sectors are obviously not on a level playing field. The handloom sector can never compete with the powerloom sector in mass production, pricing, design and market penetration. Handmade textiles are rare and considered luxury items across the world. There is a need to have a separate policy for handloom and craft sector which are niche products requiring access and penetration to niche segmented markets. Thailand has successfully marketed its 'Thai Silk' as an aspirational product. India needs to market its handmade textiles in a similar manner. India is the only country where handmade textiles are created daily by 16 million craftsmen but it has not been successful in marketing these crafts. Government should promote handmade textiles as a part of the 'creative economy' or 'cultural economy' of the country and position it accordingly in the economic goods basket on offer as export to the outside world or a niche domestic market. It has to be thus given tax concessions of an export-oriented MSME unit. Hence, handlooms need to have a separate National Handloom Policy and be taken out of the omnibus National Textile Policy. As a corollary, handloom sector could be shifted either to the Ministry of Commerce or to the Ministry of Micro, Small and Medium Enterprises (MSME). Government should automatically include handloom industry under MSME to avail the benefits of the Aatma Nirbhar Bharat scheme.

While the above measures would fructify in the medium term, the unprecedented pandemic crisis requires long term solutions. To this end, I mooted a Parliamentary Advocacy Group on Handlooms and Handicrafts in an attempt to draw the attention of Indians and the world at large to the cultural heritage that the handloom/handicraft sector embodies, support the sector and alter the discourse around artisans and weavers to bring them to the center stage of India's creative economy. It is a non-partisan group of Members of Parliament from across the country.

In August 2021, members of the Advocacy Group attended the Parliament house by wearing traditional handloom/handicrafts outfits from their respective regions to commemorate National Handloom Day. Events like this have granted visibility to the issues plaguing the sector and provided sufficient momentum to the government for taking necessary actions. This is reflected in the newly constituted Committee by the Textile Ministry tasked with strategic and policy formation for the growth of the sector. I am optimistic that collective advocacy led by the Parliamentary Advocacy Group and the Committee constituted by the government will succeed in resuscitating the handloom industry.

6.14 Caste census needs to be undertaken

The constitutional amendment 2021 restoring the power of the states to identify Socially and Economically Backward Castes (SEBCs) and Other Backward Castes (OBCs) continues to create a lot of buzz across the nation much beyond the simple clarifications inserted through the amendment.

The ceiling limit issue

However, the amendment is silent on breaching the cap of 50% on reservations as was laid down in the landmark case of Indra Sawhney and others vs Union of India and others in 1992. The amendment was necessitated after the judgment of the Supreme Court in the Maratha reservation case on Maharashtra SEBCs Reservation Act, 2018 (May 2021). However, even in this judgment, the Supreme Court re-emphasised the need for scientifically collected quantifiable data to consider revisiting the ceiling issue. The court, referring to the judgments in M Nagaraj v. UoI (2006) and Ashoka Kumar Thakur v. UoI (2008), interpreted the ratio of these cases to imply, 'If a state wants to exceed 50% reservation, then it is required to base its decision on quantifiable data.' Earlier, in the M Nagaraj case, the court had laid down that the '... the state has to collect quantifiable data showing backwardness of the class and inadequacy of representation of that class in public employment in addition to compliance of Article 335.' Therefore, if we want to get the ceiling limit increased beyond 50% through a judicial order, it can be done only through a scientifically designed survey; every other argument has no evidentiary value in the eyes of the courts.

Lacunae in the Indra Sawhney judgment

Many have argued that the judgment of the Supreme Court in the Indra Sawhney case is inherently contradictory. The court held that Article 16(1) and Article 16(4) of the Constitution were facets of the same principle guaranteeing 'substantive equality', which includes existing structural and institutional disadvantages. However, the court also affirmed the rule that there must be a 50% cap on reservation subject to 'extraordinary circumstances'.

In the judgment, there is no clear rationale as to how the court arrived at the quantification of 50%, aside from the iteration that it was a 'reasonable and fair' figure considering the aim of adequate representation and not proportional representation based on caste. The court also did not lay out the rationale behind the primacy of the doctrine of adequacy over the doctrine of proportionality.

Policy rationale behind caste-based enumeration in Census

No legislation can bring actual substantive benefits to the OBCs and the SEBCs unless we ascertain 'who' (identify) these benefits will accrue to and 'how many' (total number) of them will need to be covered under its ambit. The latest amendment answers the 'who' part of the question as the states will identify the castes to be treated as OBC/SEBC.

However, it is silent on the 'how many' question. This ambiguity can be removed only if there is data that reflects the percentage of people that need this reservation as was also noted by the courts. It is only then that one can assess if the 50% ceiling is required to be breached in order to formulate a rational reservation policy based on the doctrine of adequacy, if not proportionality. India last witnessed a comprehensive caste census last in 1931.

Focusing on the need for such a census purely from a public policy imperative, the Cabinet of Odisha passed a resolution on 11 January 2020 for the conduct of a socio-economic caste enumeration simultaneously with the General Census 2021 by adding extra columns to the existing format. The state also approached the Centre with this demand, which it refused.

However, Odisha's Naveen Patnaik became the first CM in the country to go ahead with such an enumeration from 1 May 2021, committed in his resolve to not only use such data for possibly breaching the 50% ceiling in reservations by substantially complying with the judicial order, but also ensuring that the benefits from government schemes actually reach the intended beneficiaries from the OBC and SEBC categories in a more targeted and focused manner.

The current reliance on the SEBC survey of 2011 used for estimating the number of beneficiaries under various schemes of the government relating to food security, housing, health, etc., often compels states to demand additional quota requirements from the Centre since the 2011 data is old and leaves out many eligible beneficiaries. The latter leads to a lot of avoidable politicking based on which party is in power at the Centre vis-a-vis the demanding state.

Conclusion

The jurisprudence of reservation is in the nature of affirmative action. First, it aims to abolish the past inhuman discrimination and second, it aims to mitigate suffering and mend the generational damage to these communities.

The extent to which reservations will be excessive so as to render them adverse must depend on the adequacy of representation in a particular case. This could be different in different states. Hence, fixing an upper limit of 50% for all states across the country is untenable. It is equally untenable to demand relaxation of this limit without collection of scientific, ground-level quantifiable data. Therefore, the government must heed Odisha's demand and incorporate a separate column for enumeration of OBCs and SEBCs in the forthcoming Census.

CHAPTER 7

ENVIRONMENT PROTECTION

7.1 Problems with Environment Impact Assessment

According to Nobel-winning economist Joseph Stieglitz, 'If growth is not sustainable because we are destroying the environment and using up scarce natural resources, our statistics (GDP) should warn us; it is clear that something is fundamentally wrong with the way we assess economic performance and social performance.' The battle with the current pandemic has shown us how vulnerable and unstable our systems of production, distribution and supply are in the face of Nature. The apex court had observed in Vellore Citizens Welfare Forum v Union of India (1996) that though companies are vital for the development of countries, the doctrine of 'sustainable development' must be adopted by them as a balancing concept.

The draft Environment Impact Assessment (EIA) notification 2020 to replace the EIA notification 2006 has been put in the public domain by the Ministry of Environment, Forest and Climate Change (MOEF&CC) since March 12, 2020. It has left both environmentalists as well as well-meaning economists worried if the government would throw caution completely to the wind to make good the GDP loss to the economy due to the prolonged lockdown and thus, make a mockery of its commitment to the global community made in the United Nations Climate Change Conference 2019 (COP 25).

Bypassing NGT orders

The United Nations Environment Program (UNEP) defines EIA as a tool to identify the environmental, social and economic impacts of a project prior to decision-making. The National Green Tribunal (NGT) has also consistently ruled against post-facto approvals. The new 2020 notification, however, does away with this cardinal principle of prior environment clearance and permits post facto regularisation of environment violations by paying fines so long as the project is permissible in the area. This militates against the bedrock of India's environment outlook that is based on the 'precautionary principle'. Any shift from the 'polluter-pays-principle' to the 'pollute-and-pay' principle would wreak havoc. This window was hitherto not available in the 2006 notification.

A more balanced approach would be to incentivise pre-commissioning compliance and impose extremely stiff penalties for seeking regularisation after commissioning.

Public scrutiny being compromised

In the new dispensation, public consultation, in vogue since 1997, is proposed to be exempted for a number of public projects in the field of irrigation, comprehensive area development, inland waterways, etc., or those involving 'other strategic considerations' as determined by the Centre. While these specified projects would require prior-environment clearance from the ministry, no information relating to such projects shall be placed in the public domain.

This is inexplicable considering that they are public infrastructure projects and meant for the very public from whom this information is sought to be hidden. This also flies in the face of international environmental law and agreements like the Stockholm Declaration 1972, the Rio Declaration 1992 or COP 25, which have held transparency to be the cornerstone of any climate discussion. The CAG Report of 2016 had observed that the concerns of the local people as emerging from public hearings were not being included in the final EIA reports and the project proponents did not fulfil their commitments in a time-bound manner. Instead of addressing these issues, the new draft provides further leeway to these perpetrators. Further, there may be apprehension that the government could keep any project out of any public scrutiny under the guise of 'other strategic considerations'.

Other areas that raise concern

The new law also proposes to declare some areas as 'economically sensitive areas', on the recommendation of MOEF & CC, which would then be taken outside the ambit of the mandatory environmental and other clearances. But such a declaration would be sans any public or stakeholder consultation. This could pose a serious threat to delicate and highly unstable ecosystems like sacred groves, remnant forest patches and those that sustain critically endangered fauna like the great Indian bustard, Asiatic lion and one-horned rhinoceros. Our attempt to increase our ranking in the 'ease of doing business' index might irrevocably damage our environment in the long run.

Besides, the draft notification has not paid any heed to the 2016 CAG report that revealed serious inadequacies in monitoring by third-party agencies. Out of 216 projects, the terms of reference could be granted within the prescribed time limit of 60 days only in 14% of the projects; in others there were delays up to 365 days.

The draft increases the validity of the environment clearances to 50 years for mining projects as against 30 years in the current law and 15 years for river valley projects as against 10 years, thus increasing the risk of irreversible environmental, social and health consequences on account of the project remaining unnoticed for long.

Conclusion

At COP 25, India had exhibited its seriousness and steadfast approach to tackle climate change. This new draft would come as a major embarrassment to the country in the international stage. It is also pertinent to note that India ranked a very lowly 177 out of 180 countries in the last released Environment Performance Index (EPI) 2018, a biennial report prepared by Yale and Columbia Universities along with the World Economic Forum. India must draw inspiration from countries like Singapore and Denmark that consistently top the charts in both ease of doing business and environment performance indices.

7.2 From the Pandemic to the Paris Agreement: 'Circular' to avoid a great divergence

Just as COVID-19 has wrecked havoc on the economy and there

is strong apprehension that it will have serious consequences on the environment as well since countries are starting to restore and recover fast to their pre-pandemic GDP growth parameters and other metric. A significant effort on the end of the countries would be to watch its human impact on climate. The 2015 Paris Climate Agreement along with its rules and procedures has had little to no effect on the rising concentrations of green house emissions in the atmosphere. After witnessing an initial dip, emissions are heading to pre-pandemic levels as economies around the world strive towards recovery. A watchdog of the World Meteorological Organization (WMO), the Global Atmosphere Watch (GAW) Programme, outlined that the restrictions imposed due to COVID are stated to have caused a dip in emission levels ranging between 4-7% as against the data statistics of 2019[1] which would affect the annual growth margin rate by only 0.08 ppm to 0.23 ppm. This is grossly insufficient to improve things. The latest report of the Intergovernmental Panel on Climate Change (IPCC) 2021 warned against extreme heat waves, floods, droughts and other significant environment changes if greenhouses emissions were not curbed. The report is being referred to as 'code red for humanity.'

Post Pandemic recovery structure viz. the Circular Economy Model

Recovery post pandemic needs to rely on measures that are targeted towards making climate and environment a priority while strategizing for economic recovery at the same time.

1 Data derived from the Global Carbon Project

'Green Recovery' model was asserted by the IMF and the World Bank in their post pandemic recovery policy suggestions. An impactful transition towards this would be the adoption of the circular economy model. NITI Aayog, the principal think tank of the Government, recently proposed the need to adopt the circular economy model to achieve sustainable growth. This model facilitates the elimination of waste and propagates the continued use of available resources. Designed on the principles of regeneration of natural systems, this model focuses on empowering the renewable energy resources available at hand. For example, infrastructure projects must be streamlined to identify new value streams so as to marginally cut down the carbon content that is embedded in our projects.

Another significant aspect could be to challenge the infrastructure sector to formulate designs minus the 'dispose' element of the linear model of business. This can be achieved by encouraging innovation in the early stages of the projects by structuring designs that rely on green sources of energy that are renewable. What is also imperative is our understanding of the value of 'waste.' For example, economies can venture into establishing and developing markets that use agricultural and consumer waste streams as an alternative to building materials, promoting markets that sell remanufactured or refashioned products, etc.

Another option that must be explored is the extension of support to green policies and incentives by providing rebates and guarantees. Additionally, keeping a tab on polluting energy sources is just as essential as amplifying investments into renewables.

Energy the clean way

Clean energy would enable the much needed paradigm shift from the dependence of imported fuels inclusive of their financial and environmental costs to cleaner and naturally occurring alternatives. These resources also cut down on extraction costs thereby reducing the final costs of procurement. 18 million net new jobs will be created by 2030 as a result of this transition[2]. While it would facilitate new jobs, it must also be borne in mind that it will come at some human costs which would require support for workers with social protection, re-skilling and up-skilling to ensure a clean switch. Carbon transmission, fossil fuel subsidies, coal powered resources must be forfeited. The tax structure should be rearranged from income to carbon, from taxpayers to polluters; bank lending be relooked with net zero objective; climate-related financial risk disclosures be made obligatory; and the goal of carbon neutrality (net zero) be amalgamated into all economic and fiscal decision-making.

Emission targets and Green Recovery

The Emissions Gap in 2030 is estimated at 12-15 Gigatonnes (GT) CO_{2e} to limit global warming to below 2°C and 29-32 GT CO_{2e} to limit it below 1.5°C goal. On paper this looks like a long shot, but if crucial and concerted action across all countries and sectors are made, these targets could well be achieved. Focus must shift to renewables and energy efficiency, low carbon transportation and a subsequent phase out of coal. The blue-print for green fiscal recovery encompasses the need

---

2 https://ec.europa.eu/jrc/en/science-update/employment-energy-sector

to support zero-emission technologies and infrastructure, slash fossil fuel subsidies, ensure a no new coal plants policy, and promote nature-based solutions including large-scale landscape restoration and reforestation. 5 per cent[3] of global emissions attributed to the shipping and aviation sectors also require consideration. All sectors need to combine energy efficiency alongside ensuring a brisk progression away from fossil fuels. At the climate meeting in Glasgow in November 2021, world economies pledged to take climate action as a top priority in their post pandemic economic recovery plan to achieve the goals of sustainable living.

The way forward

Private sector and individuals have both a role to play in combating climate change. Changes in consumption behaviour by both these players will be decisive. An effective and efficient step in this direction would be adoption of the circular economy model. A switch from the linear 'make-use-dispose' model to the circular 'reuse' model would help build economic, natural, and social capital via renewable energy resources. Circular economy would, alongside providing environmental and societal benefits also generate opportunities for business and economic growth. The pandemic has taught us that we need sustainable living now more than ever before. We owe it to the generations to come. Climate change can no longer be at the rear end of things; it needs to take the centre-stage.

3 Emissions Gap Report 2020

CHAPTER 8

WOMEN EMPOWERMENT

8.1 Women in workforce

According to the 2018 Periodic Labour Force Survey (PLFS), 22% of women in India above 15 years of age were part of the labour force, as against 71.2% men between July 2017 and June 2018. In Nordic countries, almost three in four working-age women are part of the paid labour force. This rate is currently 46.8% in the US, 47.3% in Canada and 48% in France. India lags far behind countries like China (61%), Vietnam (73%), Singapore (60%), Bangladesh (36%) and Pakistan (24%). Ironically, soon after the Covid-19 lockdown kicked in, the country, particularly in states like Odisha and Kerala, experienced the productivity and resoluteness of women force in its fight against the pandemic, be it in making masks, gloves and sanitisers, door-to-door vegetables retailing in containment areas, and distributing dry ration and cooked food to vulnerable households. They also spread awareness among communities about preventive protocols for breaking the chain of the virus.

All the work they did would ordinarily have been conducted in the formal sector as a paid service, and counted as an output of the labour force. Except that most of their work is counted as being in the informal sector and, therefore, not counted as labour output. While this may be a technical issue of economic statistics, it is an eye-opener about women in rural areas who can be brought into the labour force by organising them into self-help groups (SHGs), and by promoting micro-entrepreneurial activities among them.

The patriarchal family structure, lack of education and required skills, restriction to household chores, lack of access to a safe workplace, maternity benefit and gender gap in pay are some reasons that deter women to participate in India's labour force. GoI's ambitious 'Startup India, Stand Up India' campaign has also failed to attract women entrepreneurs without government-guaranteed credit support.

The Odisha government's Mission Shakti movement launched in 2001 involving seven million rural women has been successfully organised into about six lakh women SHGs. Another success story is of Kudumbashree, the Kerala state poverty eradication mission launched in 1998, which covers 4.39 million women into about three lakh SHGs.

In both cases, financial assistance is provided to these SHGs through extremely soft bank loans to encourage them to take up various self-employment works and micro projects. This explains a higher level of female participation in the labour force in Kerala compared to other states.

Recently, the Odisha government went a step further and tied them to a marketing support of Rs 5,000 crore in the next five years through government procurement systems such as

PDS, midday meals and other nutrition support programmes besides medical supplies and infrastructure maintenance works.

Thus, an appropriate ecosystem promoting formation of such women SHGs, empowered by basic vocational training in low technology-intensive micro enterprises like making candles and masks, tailoring, driving and computer literacy on the lines of 'Skill India' is the only way to bring women into the labour force, though still in the informal sector. This is one important take away from the Covid-19 lockdown.

8.2 The Motherhood Penalty and Female Labour Force Participation in India

A large part of India still treats its women as inferior to men, with socially entrenched notions of patriarchy continuing to be dominant. This is evident from India's 2021 Global Gender Gap Index rankings, wherein it has slipped 28 places, compared to 2020 (rank 140 out of 156 nations). The gender gap in the country has also widened to 62.5%, with especially low gender parity in political empowerment and economic participation and opportunity. Women are paid considerably less than men, with some research (from the Avtar Group) showing that the gender pay gap between women and men in the same jobs with equivalent qualifications can be as much as 34%. India, as of 2020, has the lowest female labour force participation rates even amongst the South Asian nations, with four out of five women not working.

Motherhood Penalty

Amongst women, mothers face higher discrimination compared to non-mothers. Correll et al (2007) have found that employers perceive mothers as being less competent and committed compared to non-mothers and hold them to much higher professional standards. They are also hired and promoted less often and generally receive lower salaries. Thus, women with children are punished professionally. This is otherwise called 'motherhood penalty.'

The motherhood penalty in India has been documented by Das and Zumbyte (2017) using a logit regression to establish an increasingly negative relationship between the probability of Indian women getting employed, and the presence of a young child in their households. Bedi et al (2018) conducted a field experiment in India, wherein they sent fake CVs for service sector jobs, with some CVs selected at random to include mothers and found the presence of a motherhood penalty in the call back rates for these applications. Mothers are employed lesser than non-mothers, implying that the motherhood penalty plays a significant role in low Indian female labour force participation, which according to World Bank data, 2020, is only 20.3%.

Impact of the Pandemic

The pandemic has exacerbated the gender divide with women, and consequently mothers, suffering much more than men. According to OXFAM, 17 million women lost their jobs in April 2020, with unemployment rates rising to 15.8% compared with 12.6% amongst men in September 2020. Women were found to be seven times more likely to lose their jobs in the lockdown phases, and if rendered unemployed, were eleven times more likely to remain unemployed, as compared to their male counterparts. A potential reason for this is the increased burden of domestic responsibilities that the average Indian woman has to bear - with schools closing, an increase in elderly caregiving and workplaces transitioning to a work-from-home model which has blurred the line between working hours and personal time. Even pre-pandemic, a Time Use Survey conducted by the NSSO, showed that women spent approximately 4.47 hours on childcare and other caregiving responsibilities, in contrast to the meagre 0.88 hours for men, thus rendering mothers at a much greater disadvantage.

Way Forward

To combat the motherhood penalty, reorienting workplace norms to make them more gender-equal is essential. There still exist employer notions about women returning after maternity breaks being under-skilled or having a lower productivity. Currently, India has a Maternity Benefit Act, but no similar law for paternity benefits. The amendment to the Act in 2017 increased paid maternity leave from 12 to 26 weeks. Though well-meaning, this fortifies notions of caregiving being primarily the onus of the woman and in fact, reinforces and increases the risk of women being subject to the motherhood penalty. Thus, an explicit and formalised act for mandatory paternity benefits will go a long way towards equalizing gender roles and reducing employer bias.

Furthermore, the provision and strengthening of childcare facilities for working mothers are extremely important. The Maternity Benefit Act mandates the setting up of crèche facilities for organizations with more than 50 employees. But majority of states are yet to frame and notify rules under the Act, which contributes to its low compliance. A better policy measure would be to provide mothers requiring childcare with a monthly allowance. This would have also helped mothers working from home during the pandemic, by allowing them to avail themselves of alternate childcare methods.

While paternity benefits and better childcare will partially alleviate the motherhood penalty, the problem of the gender pay gap that women and mothers face remains unsolved. The Code on Wages, 2019 puts the responsibility of detection and punishment of non-compliance with the inspector. However, it has been argued that the onus of compliance should be on the employer, as opposed to third parties such as inspectors. Iceland, the most gender-equal nation, pioneered a policy in 2018 that requires firms with more than 25 employees to prove they provide equal pay every three years. When proven, these companies receive certification, which has been made mandatory since the beginning of 2020. All companies without certification incur a daily fine. This shift of the burden of proof to the employer has been reported to have improved the workplace environment, and increased female employee trust in employers. Ireland is another example that requires companies with more than 250 employees to publish data on disparities between average and median hourly wages and bonuses for both genders as well as the differences in the percentage of men and women that receive benefits-in-kind.

Conclusion

For India, adopting the Icelandic policy of mandatory certification would be beneficial. A specific committee, with at least half the members being female, should be instituted for the review of documents of proof submitted by firms, and to ensure sanctions are imposed on non-compliant employers. Mandated publishing of data on disparities in wages between the two genders would also compel firms to pay equally since wage disparities could harm their reputation. This would help mitigate the gender pay gap in the nation - and consequently, the pay gap associated with the motherhood penalty.

8.3 Utilizing SHGs to help curb domestic violence

Amid the Covid-19 lockdown around the world, there has been an unhealthy surge of violence against women in many countries, weighing down local law enforcement. Globally, the figure of affected women could easily cross over an estimate of 30 million in the next six months, according to the United Nations. In India alone, the complaints received by the National Commission for Women have doubled to 257 complaints in the first 10 days of the lockdown, as compared to 116 complaints registered in the first week of March, 2020.

Stock responses and strategies

Over the years, the key strategic response of countries pertaining to domestic violence has been heavy criminalisation of offences by laying down stringent punitive measures and penalties on the abuser. However, such strong coercive measures against gender-related offences cannot be a standalone solution to tackling the complex issue of crimes against women. According to Dr Prabha Kotiswaran, Professor of Law and Social Justice at King's College London, harsher laws seem to be a poor deterrent. As in any other law, the certainty of punishment has a bigger deterrent impact. The Protection of Women from Domestic Violence Act (PWDVA) was envisaged initially as a civil remedy against issues of domestic violence, as the certainty of punishment is low and trials are harder on victims.

There is increasing evidence in several nations and experiences of civil societies that interventions to bring about behavioural change in the abuser at a culture-cognitive level has been an effective supportive strategy in tackling gender-related violence. In India, the legislation for addressing domestic violence is victim-centred in its approach, weighing heavily towards criminalisation under section 498-A of the Indian Penal Code with little thrust on engagement with the perpetrators. However, considering the peculiar situation of the victims being compelled to stay within the same confines as the abuser due to lockdown and their inability to run out to police stations to file complaints due to restrictions on movement, there were calls for declaring all services under the Protection of Women from Domestic Violence Act (PWDVA) as 'essential' besides having separate shelter homes and psychological support for the survivors. This was unprecedented.

There was also a call for exploring the possibility of involving the perpetrators in the process of prevention of these gender atrocities by extending reformative measures to them. The practices of engagement with men in efforts to prevent violations can take place in primarily two ways: by introducing therapeutic intervention and by encouraging men's participation in programmes denouncing gender-related violence.

In the context of the first approach, the scope of extending counselling services to offenders is very limited under the PWDVA Act in India. Such measures are targeted only towards women, but it does little to change the household environment in which she could be stuck with the perpetrator and his family members during the lockdown. The practical realities regarding available redressal systems on the ground appear to be grim given the lack of human resources, police personnel, and the inadequate number of shelter homes.

The second approach focuses on the prevention of violence before it occurs by engaging men in awareness-raising programmes through campaigns on social media and television. Civil societies and quasi-state interventions have increasingly adopted these methods. Their experience suggests that sensitisation measures with men and young boys have been effective in deterring atrocities against women.

Towards a gender-just society

While the emphasis on criminal liability in legislations has been efficacious in ensuring deterrence of atrocities, a gender-just society could be achieved when masses collectively condemn violence towards women. This vision can come true with policy-backing to programmes, creating behavioural change in the perpetrators, leading to unlearning of deeply ingrained patriarchal beliefs, especially with offenders. Counselling services, a key part of the state's response mechanism to the aggrieved woman, should also be made mandatory for perpetrators throughout the period of lockdown.

In rural areas, already proven community models such as women-led self-help groups, village-level community-based organisations and community courts could be leveraged for mandatory counselling of the perpetrators, resolution of conflicts, psychological support, and creation of sensitisation around the issue. This could be helpful in easing stress and tension in the household since community-based surveillance can be real-time, continuous, and brings in ownership of the entire community to this exercise rather than just the affected family.

8.4 Women in temple boards—All male monopolies

In a groundbreaking move in 2020, for the first time in its 45-year history, the Saptashrung Gad Trust appointed a woman trustee on the board of Shree Saptashrung Niwasini Devi Temple in Maharashtra. In 2016, the trust board of Shani Shingnapur Temple appointed its first woman president. But there is little to rejoice because these are exceptional cases and the majority of temples in India lack appropriate representation of women in managerial boards. Ayodhya Temple being the an example where all the 15 trustees are male. It is quite dismaying since women have been the marginalised gender facing religious discrimination from eternity.

Legal position

The composition and appointment of trustees are usually governed under the respective state Hindu Religious Institutions and Charitable Endowments (HR&CE) legislation. States like Kerala, Tamil Nadu and Karnataka have laws mandating reservation for women on the Board of Trustees. Andhra Pradesh is the latest entrant (in 2019) where women have been given 50 per cent reservation in the temple committees. Inclusion of women in temple committees was one of the most significant promises of the election campaign of Chief Minister Y.S. Jagan Mohan Reddy.

Laws of many states like Puducherry and Odisha do not

prescribe reservation for women in the temple committees. Although Tamil Nadu provides reservation for women in the Board of Trustees, it does not lay down such a provision in case of state-level advisory committee. The committee is constituted under the Tamil Nadu Hindu Religious and Charitable Endowments Act 1959 to advise and guide the state government on the matters of temple administration. Absence of women at the highest level of decision-making is disappointing.

Apart from the HR&CE legislation, temples are also governed under individual temple Acts. The Puri Jagannath Temple in Odisha has a special law called Shri Jagannath Puri Act 1955, which stipulates the superintendence, control and management of the temple. These functions are carried out by Shri Jagannath Temple Managing Committee, but the Act does not incorporate provision on women in the committee. Laws governing Siddhi Vinayak Ganpati Temple in Maharashtra and Vaishno Devi shrine in Jammu and Kashmir also suffer from a similar omission.

Amongst the Muslims, the Waqf Act 1995 mandates women representation under Section 14 of the Act. Likewise, the Golden Temple administered by the Shiromani Gurdwara Parbandhak Committee under the Sikh Gurdwara Act 1925 provides women with the right to vote and election to the committee.

Current status

Barring Kerala, even in states mandating reservation the proportion of women in temple administration is extremely low. For instance, Tamil Nadu HR&CE department has not appointed the Board of Trustees in the past five years. In its absence, a 'fit person' has been tasked with the responsibilities of the Board, and such a person is usually a male. Like temples, the position of women in the administration of mosques and Gurudwara is also not very encouraging. (The information was last updated on 19 Feb, 2021)

Patriarchy and power behind exclusion

Central to the exclusion of women from religious spaces is the idea of the impurity of a woman and a patriarchal perspective that sexualises the very presence of a woman, demeaning her to the status of a mere seductress who will corrupt the holy men. The tale of Eve, who ushers in the fall of mankind by lewdly seducing Adam into sin, is a recurrent theme across various religions. A historical lens, as adopted by feminist anthropologists such as Janice Delaney, Mary Jane Lupton, and Emily Toth, points towards the introduction of the idea of 'impurity' as a tool to reinforce male supremacy, especially in relation to a woman's menstrual cycle. The stance is hypocritical.

While the Vedas revere menstrual blood as the 'giver of life', religious spaces have often used women's biology as a tool to disempower and exclude them from religion. Strange as it may sound, the festival 'Raja Parba' celebrated in Odisha every year observes the menstruation of Mother Earth, considered equivalent to the menstrual cycle of a woman. The occasion marks the celebration of a woman's power to reproduce. It is believed that mother earth menstruates during the three-day festival. As a mark of respect towards the Earth during her menstruation days, all agricultural work comes to a standstill. Similarly, the Ambubachi Mela is an annual fair held at Kamakhya temple in Guwahati, Assam. It celebrates the menstruation course of Goddess Kamakhya.

The coexistence of pious glorification of women as embodied in 'Kali' with the misogynistic exclusion of women from performance of religion at all levels is simply a convenient narrative constructed by patriarchy. The sanctity of religious spaces is defined through sanctions on the presence of women, making women and religion apparently antithetical to each other. A further possible explanation behind this hypocrisy could be gender-based power play perpetuated by patriarchy.

Need State intervention

Amid the controversial temple entry cases, talk about uniform civil code and the frequent debates around women empowerment, the State should make it mandatory for every religious institution to give adequate representation to women. Unlike the legislative and executive branch of the government, the issue of women reservation in temple committees is gaining momentum in the judiciary. In 2018, the Supreme Court heard a plea seeking inclusion of woman in the management of the historic Trimbakeshwar Shiva Temple in Maharashtra. Thus, there is an underlying need to dismantle gender stereotypes attached to religion. Doing so can provide the legitimate right and liberty to Indian women.

CHAPTER 9

TRANSGENDERS RIGHTS

9.1 India needs holistic implementation of laws for LGBTQ+ community

In a unique initiative, the Noida Metro Rail Corporation (NMRC) decided in June 2020 to convert Aqua Line's Sector 50 Metro station into a 'She-Man' station in order to promote transgender rights. It also plans to include members of the transgender community at ticket counters and other areas of the station. In June 2020, Assam became the first state in the country to form a welfare board exclusively for transgenders.

Much earlier, in 2016, Odisha had become the first state in the country to give transgender people social welfare benefits such as a pension, housing and food grains—usually allocated for only the most impoverished and those living below the poverty line (BPL). This includes free housing, 100 days of paid work annually, pensions and loans to start their own businesses. They are also entitled to 5 kg of food grains every month under the National Food Security Act, 2013. Similarly, in 2020, in another progressive gesture, the Bhubaneswar Municipal Corporation (BMC) roped in members from the transgender community to collect pending property taxes of around Rs 11 crore. In Rourkela, they were drafted as Corona Warriors.

As per Census 2011, there are 4.9 lakh transgenders in India. On April 16, 2020, the Indian transgender community celebrated six years of the landmark judgment of the Supreme Court in National Legal Services Authority (NALSA) vs Union of India, wherein the apex court recognised the right of transgenders to self-determine their gender identity. Two days later, on April 18, 2020, the Government of India released the draft rules on transgender rights in the exercise of the powers conferred on it by sub-section (1) and (2) of Section 22 of the historic Transgender Persons (Protection of Rights) Act, 2019 (parent law) passed by the Indian Parliament in November 2019.

While some stark anomalies in the law have been pointed out by activists and experts, particularly relating to the additional requirement of a certificate from the District Magistrate so as to be officially recognised as 'transgender,' coalescing diverse trans identities like persons with intersex variations, gender, queer and persons with socio-cultural identities as *kinner*, *hijra*, *aravanai* and *jogta* into one umbrella and not aligning provisions in IPC (for crimes relating to sexual and physical abuse) and several other bi-gender laws with the new transgender law, a number of issues relating to operationalising even the existing law as enacted remain.

Issues in Operationalisation of Education

There are no provisions that mention how people from the community are to be protected from discrimination and humiliation in schools and other educational institutes.

Transgender students experience resentment, prejudice and threatening environments in schools, which leads to significant dropout rates, with very few transgender people advancing to higher education. There are no reservations for their higher education prospects either.

Employment

Transgender individuals in India often face stigma and systematic exclusion in employment. This takes many forms and can include termination, failure to hire, demotion, and hostile work environment among others. There is no provision for separate toilets for them either in educational institutions or in offices and they are not allowed entry into the regular toilets meant for men and women. No comprehensive law exists yet to put an end to all such issues. Workplace-related research on lesbian, gay, bisexual and trans (LGBT) individuals reveals that transgender workers are the most marginalised and are excluded from gainful employment, with discrimination occurring at all phases of the employment process, including recruitment, training opportunities, employee benefits, and access to job advancement. Unemployment, low-paying and high-risk, and unstable jobs feed into the cycle of poverty and homelessness. As a result, some feel they have no alternative but to turn to sex work. HIV prevalence among India's transgender community is twenty six times higher than the national rate and at the same time, it is difficult to access healthcare without facing discrimination.

Housing

The Centre has failed to address the most basic issue faced by the trans-community vis-à-vis housing. Sexual orientation or gender identity is nowhere specified as protected classes for availing the benefits of Centre/State-funded housing initiatives. Many times, landlords do not let their houses on rent to transgender people for fear of drawing social stigma and consternation.

Public spaces

This is another area where transgender people commonly encounter discrimination. Public spaces include everything from restaurants to shops to banks—and people can experience humiliating treatment in these environments. There is no central law prohibiting sex discrimination in such public accommodations. Most transgender people are in very bad condition because of social exclusion.

There is a lack of sensitivity regarding the issues that people from the LGBTQ+ community face. The mere recognition of their community as the third gender is not sufficient. Laws must ensure that their community is holistically accepted in the fabric of Indian society.

The international community's recent commitment to Sustainable Development Goals (SDGs) presents an opportunity to catalyse and expand positive interventions. The SDGs are guided by the UN Charter and grounded in the Universal Declaration of Human Rights (UDHR). They reiterate universal respect for human rights and dignity, justice and non-discrimination, and a world of equal opportunity permitting the full realisation of human potential for all irrespective of race, colour, sex, language, religion, political or other opinions, national or social origin, property, birth, disability, or other status. India is a member of the UDHR and needs a holistic implementation of laws for the LGBTQ+ community that actually relieves them of their real struggles.

9.2 Transgender Rights under Threat

April 16th 2020, the transgender community celebrated six years of the landmark judgment of the Supreme Court in National Legal Services Authority (NALSA) vs Union of India WP (Civil) No 400 of 2012 wherein the Apex Court recognised the right to self-determine gender identity and directed the government to come up with an all-inclusive law for protection of rights and welfare of transgender people. Two days later on 18th April 2020, the Government of India decided to release the draft rules on transgender rights in exercise of the powers conferred by sub-section (1) and (2) of Section 22 the Transgender Persons (Protection of Rights) Act, 2019 (parent law). A law apparently put in place for protection of the community does little to uphold their rights and respect their individuality. This essay talks about how the current draft rules published, further falls short of the expectations of the trans-community. It is imperative here to note that within one month of the parent law being brought into force, a petition was taken to the Supreme Court by Assam's first transgender judge, Swati Bidhan Baruah, arguing that several provisions in the Act itself went against the dignity of the transgender people. The matter is currently *sub judice*.

Brief History

At the onset we must first delve into the SC judgement that paved the way for transgender rights in India. As held in this judgement, transgender people have the right to be treated equally under the Constitution of India, they have the right to self-identification, identifying one's gender as male, female, or third gender, and predominantly recognising them as socially and economically backward classes, thereby making them eligible for reservations in jobs and educational institutions.

Anomalies in the draft rules

Firstly, on a bare perusal of the draft rules, there are various provisions that raise concerns. The need to submit a report from a psychologist to obtain the certificate of identity under Rule 4 is in contrast to the provisions of the parent law and the NALSA judgment. The Act categorically provided in Section 4 for a right to self-perceived gender identification and said the person could apply to District Magistrate for an identification document that certifies such status. The rules proposed for the Act, however, seek for consultation with a psychologist too.

Besides being in clear violation of the Supreme Court ruling, these provisions are also contrary to international standards for legal gender recognition. International standards and best practices – including those of multiple United Nations agencies, the World Medical Association, and the World Professional Association for Transgender Health – call for separation of legal and medical processes of gender reassignment for transgender people. This includes the removal of evaluations of applicants for legal gender recognition by panels of psychologists, physicians, or other experts. Self-declared identity for transgenders should form the basis for access to all social security measures, benefits, and entitlements. Secondly, under Section 6 of the parent law, the certificate of identity can only record the gender as 'transgender'. The same is reflected in the rule 5 of the draft published. Coalescing of diverse identities into one 'transgender' umbrella encroaches upon the dignity of individuals and is against traditions of the transgender community in various parts of India. This irregularity sought legislative sanction from the definition of the term 'transgender' in the parent law. The Act defines a transgender person as 'a person whose gender does not match with the gender assigned to that person at birth and includes trans-man or trans-woman, person with intersex variations, gender queer and person having such socio-cultural identities as kinner, hijra, aravani and jogta.' Providing a single bracket of 'transgender' for inclusion of all members of the LGBTQ+ community is disrespecting and inconsiderate to say the least. The law should be more sensitive and provide for a separate schedule that needs to be annexed which identifies the various social-cultural identities for what they really are. The fact that both the Act and the draft rules merge transgender people with intersex people proves that it wasn't thoroughly thought through. Not every intersex person identifies as transgender, and not every transgender person is intersex.

Lastly, rule 6 provides for the procedure for obtaining an identity certificate for change of gender under Section 7 of the parent law. This new rules indicates the revised gender of the transgender persons post Sex Reassignment Surgery (SRS) as either male or female. This takes us back to the old notion of bigenderism. This provision could actually make the decade long movements for transgender rights look futile as it is in complete ignorance of the sentiments of the transgender community to wish to be acknowledged and identified as respective citizens without having to lose their real identity. This also raises ambiguity as to the entitlement of such persons to receive the benefits of the government for the transgender persons because their revised identity cards would categorise them as either male or female. Critiques who vouch for a different stand must remember that gender, being genetically hardwired into brain, is not subject to reassignment. It can at best be affirmed by bringing the external appearance (sex) of the person to become congruent with their gender. Transsexuals going in for SRS must be separately recognised as trans-men for those undergoing female to male transition and trans-women for those undergoing male to female transition. This will thereby ensure that the provisions in the law granted to transgenders for their empowerment could also be availed by those who wish to go for sex reassignment surgeries. This is specially to be taken care of since in spite of surgeries, most transgenders still go through gender dysphoria.

Amendments that need incorporation

The parent law along with the draft rules is silent on civil rights such as marriage, civil partnership and adoption, as well as rights to succession, inheritance and property. The NALSA judgment had specifically noted the widespread discrimination suffered by transgender persons due to the binary notion of gender in laws relating to marriage, divorce, adoption, inheritance, succession, taxation and welfare. Our lawmakers need to provide for the said discrepancies along with following a more humane and sensitized approach to deal with the issues that persist in the LGBTQ+ community. It is imperative to note that the violence and harassment directed at transgender persons is not just an affront to individual rights, but reflects the deep rooted societal prejudice and contempt towards the community as a whole.

The 2020 episode of the Kerala student Anjana dying in Goa puts focus on inhuman 'conversion therapy' on queer people. Another lacuna in the current law followed by the draft rules is the 'offences and penalties' section (Section 18), which establishes that the maximum punishment for crimes against trans-persons, including sexual and physical abuse, will be two years along with an unspecified fine. In comparison to this, for crimes against women such as stalking (Indian Penal Code 354D) and sexual harassment (IPC 354A), the punishment is at least three years in jail; for rape, it is life imprisonment. There is no explanation behind this other than the unsaid assumption that the trauma experienced by trans-people is somehow less grave even when the crime is the same. The draft rules need to be amended in such a fashion so as to resist, contest and diminish the damage inflicted by the parent law.

Conclusion

The Office of the UN High Commissioner for Human Rights in 2015 had recommended that states begin immediately 'issuing legal identity documents, upon request, that reflect preferred gender, eliminating abusive preconditions.' A 2015 report by the World Health Organization and the Asia-Pacific Transgender Network recommended that governments 'take all necessary legislative, administrative, and other measures to fully recognise each person's self-defined gender identity, with no medical requirements or discrimination on any grounds.' India must take these parameters in account in reconsidering its own transgender laws. Legislative backing of systemic ambiguities enables the perpetuation of structural violence against the trans-community in India.

From poor mental health, discrimination, isolation or abuse, the root cause of most problems faced by them can be traced back to inadequate policy, which fails to provide for their special circumstances and does not adequately address the issues faced by them. India still has a long way ahead to achieve gender justice, and the transgender community wants concerted endeavours made to bring about legislative reform so that transgender people are as free and empowered in their respective lives as any other citizen of India.

9.3 Time for a revamp in law – Gender Neutrality

A petition was moved in the Supreme Court in September 2020 by Advocate Reepak Kansal seeking equal protection from sexual crimes for the transgender community under the Indian Penal Code (IPC). I too had raised this issue in the Rajya Sabha on 21st November 2019 while speaking on the occasion of consideration and passing of the Transgender Persons (Protection of Rights) Bill 2019. Clauses (i), (ii) and (iv) of sub-section (1) of Section 354A IPC (sexual harassment), sec 354B (outraging of modesty), sec 375 IPC (rape) excludes transgenders as victims of such offences which is in violation of Article 14 (Right to equality), Article 15 (Right against discrimination), and Article 21 (Right to life and personal liberty) of the Constitution of India. For a long time in history, the prevailing approach to sexual violence in international human rights instruments has focused exclusively on the abuse of women and girls. In the meantime, sexual violence against transgenders and males continues to flourish in prisons and other places. The criminal laws in India relating to rape have always been couched in gender specific terms where men have been typecast as sole perpetrators and women as sole victims of sexual offences. The Justice J.S. Verma Committee (2013), which was constituted after the infamous Nirbhaya gang rape case, recommended gender neutral rape law with respect to victims. However no such law has yet seen the light of the day.

As per statistics, one in two transgender individuals is sexually abused or assaulted at some point in their lives. Some reports estimate that transgender survivors undergo sexual assaults of up to 66 percent along with occasional physical assaults or abuse. The majority section of the transgender community is leading a life of trauma, agony, and fear. Their Right to Life with personal dignity is being constantly challenged.

Legislative enactments not keeping pace with the judiciary

The Supreme Court of India in 2014 passed a ground breaking judgement in the matter of *NALSA* v. *Union of India* (NALSA judgement) and granted recognition to the transgender/third gender as 'persons' falling under the ambit of Article 14 of the Indian Constitution. The aim behind this judicial action was to grant equity and equality to members of the transgender community and to do away with the 'second-grade citizen' status attached to them. On 5th December, 2019, the heavily debated Transgender Persons (Protection of Rights) Act, 2019 (2019 Act) received the assent of the President and came into force and became the governing law relating to transgender rights in India. It however fell remarkably short of the expectations sought to be fulfilled. Sexual abuse against transgenders was recognised as an offense however, the maximum punishment provided for the same was only two years as opposed to the offence of rape in the IPC where the maximum punishment provided is seven years. Such disparity in punishment is both condescending and discriminatory.

Due to underreporting and lack of reliable complaints mechanisms, there is no estimate on the number of rape cases reported and prosecuted against transgenders. Additionally, there are no official national statistics on the prevalence of sexual violence perpetrated against them. It is the need of the hour for an amendment of the rape law in the country to include this marginalised section of society under its ambit.

Practices from around the world

In recent years, local and national authorities in countries around the world have adopted wide ranging measures to address human rights violations against lesbian, gay, bisexual, transgender (LGBT) and intersex people. More than a hundred United Nations member states from all regions have committed to addressing violence and discrimination on the basis of sexual orientation and gender identity. In addition to enacting new laws, some States have adopted comprehensive cross-Government action plans to protect the rights of LGBT and intersex people, set up consultative bodies that include LGBT and intersex people, and partnered with civil society organisations to jointly tackle these challenges.

To effectively address and prevent violence and abuse against LGBT and intersex people, a system of law enforcement that incorporates respect for human rights and awareness of the range of issues faced by LGBT and intersex persons is needed. Furthermore, victims of violence or abuse are unlikely to come forward to report a crime unless the police are seen as a source of protection and not of additional persecution or trauma. In Denmark, members of the police force and civil society were invited to participate in hate crime awareness training as part of a European-Union-funded project, 'Tracing and Tackling Hate and Sexual Crimes against LGBT Persons'. In Belgium, the police force has set up a transgender working group, collaborated with transgender organisations and with the Federal Institute for Gender Equality and offered training to police officers on respecting the rights of transpersons, including in filing complaints and conducting police searches. Promoting acceptance and understanding of LGBT and intersex issues among law enforcement personnel through targeted training programmes is central to developing a relationship between them and the LGBT and intersex people who require their protection.

Towards a better future

Due to lack of adequate legislation, discriminatory attitudes, harassment by police, stigma, ill treatment in detention and medical settings, lack of protective legislation, absence of complaints and grievance redressal mechanisms and lack of trust in law enforcement officials coupled with lack of awareness by judicial officers resulting in impunity for perpetrators, it is difficult for LGBTQ+ community to access effective remedies and support without fear. In the recent future, India will be looking for a major overhaul of its criminal laws. There is a five-member committee, appointed by the Ministry of Home Affairs that is reviewing the recommendations to be brought to the criminal laws in the country. Here's hoping that the Indian legal system comes up with comprehensive changes to ensure that the new law promulgated promotes inclusivity, fairness, equity and removes discrimination.

CHAPTER 10

COVID 19 AND PARLIAMENT

10.1 Parliament during COVID 19

The 18-day Monsoon Session of Parliament started on September 14, 2020 with unprecedented but believed to be largely justified, precautions against the coronavirus, including staggered sittings of both Houses and social distancing between MPs.

However when the session began, there was a complete sense of dishevelment. The timings of the Houses had been shortened to four hours each and the Parliament was functioning for seven days a week.

The timings for Rajya Sabha were scheduled from 9 am to 1 pm, and the Lok Sabha from 3 pm to 7 pm. That means no morning jog, no work-out and no late nights! What stood out the most when you enter Parliament is the emptiness.

There are no milling crowds, no chatter, and no reporters tailing parliamentarians. What was most disconcerting is the implementation of the '*do gajj ki doori*' formula. Some of us were sitting in the galleries meant for visitors and in the 'blue' chamber reserved for the 'elected' MPs even though people in the Rajya Sabha are unelected.

Before the commencement of the session, the members were requested to get their RT-PCR tests conducted 72 hours prior to their appearance. If the tests were not done, then there was provision to get it done at the reception and the members were to wait till the results were out.

If the members were found coronavirus-negative, but symptomatic, their RT-PCR test was conducted and home isolation advised till the results came in. Coincidentally, the virus has a shelf life of 14 days, enough to outlive the session!

I thought this situation wouldn't arise, but it did happen. On the first day, some 25 MPs tested positive for the virus and had to be quarantined. Thermal guns and thermal scanners were being used for noting the body temperatures of all those entering the House. Each human entering the Parliament was a potential threat.

In addition, proper measures for sanitisation of the premises were also undertaken. Touch-less sanitisers were installed at 40 spots within the House and emergency medical teams and ambulances stood on standby.

The preparation is reminiscent of the sci-fi film, Contagion. Members, fully masked and some even with visors, were allowed to address the Chair while sitting in their respective seats. The problem with the masks is that it is difficult to quickly identify someone.

When I thanked one Hon'ble MP for a nice Zero Hour submission, his first reaction was 'I can't recognise you.' When I pulled the mask down, he had a toothy grin in sheepish acknowledgement of his apparent faux passé.

Each of the rows in the Lok Sabha were separated by polycarbonate sheets to ensure adequate physical distancing.

Every intervention and statement was relayed in both the chambers and the galleries. There were consoles, special cables between the two House chambers and ultraviolet germicidal irradiation to prevent infections.

A mobile application was introduced for registering attendance as well. No guests were allowed and there was restricted entry for media. On any given day, there were not more than 35 reporters allowed inside the premises.

No photographers, except from the news agency PTI, were provided access. And these camerapersons too are not allowed into the Central Hall.

There was no canteen and some good friends turning up in the Central Hall with their tiffin boxes taking you back to school. People outside think MPs have a good time.

But trust me, it isn't easy, and of course, there was the ever-lurking fear of the virus. On the first day when I sat in the gallery, I found it hot and humid only to be told that the Chairman had ordered temperature to be kept at 24-degree Celsius following doctor's advice.

The Lok Sabha chamber was more comfortable since it boasts a bigger hall and therefore air circulation is better. Everyone seemed to have an explanation for everything.

With respect to the functioning, the Zero Hour cut down to half and the Question Hour scrapped. It was a unique arrangement, a historical sitting and a life-time experience.

Despite the fear of the virus, the Lok Sabha and the Rajya Sabha were scheduled to take up 47 items (these include 45 Bills and two financial items) in 18 sittings. The show had to go on. We are after all responsible representatives. I am, however, not sure how many common citizens would have ventured to attend such a session.

10.2 Reimagining polls after COVID 19: Digital transformation a safe bet

In May 2021, the Madras and Calcutta High Courts came down heavily on the EC for conducting elections in several states where Covid-appropriate behaviour was being flagrantly violated, amidst a raging second wave of the pandemic. In 2020, during the first wave, EC had come out with 'Broad Guidelines for conduct of elections during Covid-19' after consultations with national and regional political parties. However, a close look at EC guidelines would indicate it only tapers down the strength of mass gatherings, while still retaining the basic structure of a physical election campaigning. Many of us would know it's impossible to comply with or effectively monitor these restrictions in the field.

There are several ways in which the current situation should influence for better democratic processes in the future. Firstly, the lockdown opened up several possibilities for reaching out to people through online and social media, web-based broadcasts, webcasts and webinars. It's believed that from less than 10% voters in 2014 to more than 30% voters in 2019 were influenced by social media, with more than ten times increased spending on digital campaigns. In August 2020, two events stood out as disruptive and transformative. Party workers and leaders sent messages through their Facebook, Twitter, Instagram and YouTube accounts in Congress's Speak Up campaign. And BJP started its Jan Samvad virtual rallies in every state in which nearly five lakh party workers would listen to their leader's speeches on YouTube, Facebook Live and the Namo app. These online rallies to reach out to booth level from a central place wouldn't have been possible in physical form. We can well imagine the drastic reduction in campaigning costs such online events would bring to the candidates.

Secondly, it's high time the voting process itself underwent a change with use of technology for e-voting, as going to a booth to press the same button in an EVM machine isn't medically advisable in a pandemic situation. Moreover, arrangements to organise elections with no health ramifications would require EC or governments to hire almost 30-40 lakh medical staff, purchase disinfection items and provide medical supplies to ensure safety of more than 10 lakh booths. Besides, polling invites involvement of security forces whose stay, movement and deployment costs are huge.

Questions are raised about security of an e-voting system. Although when financial data of crores of Indians can be securely kept within the banking system through use of robust technology, similar possibility may well-nigh exist for e-voting by using Aadhaar-linked, individual-voter-specific, non-transferable link and exercising voting preferences either from home or from Jan Seva Kendras (mainly for rural voters).

If this happens, one can imagine the savings that can happen in the system. Estonia has nearly perfected the e-polling system with almost 47% of the country voting online in last year's parliamentary election. The Estonian i-voting system is highly transparent and digitally secure. It preserves voter's anonymity while ensuring the right to vote with paper ballot parallel to digital voting. It's worth emulation.

Thirdly, the very basis of physical meeting of MPs and MLAs in a large space in the Parliament or legislatures should undergo a change. Elected representatives could meet virtually. Imagine the savings as there would be no travelling expenses, marshals, staff who take physical short-handnotes, canteens etc. Similarly, committee meetings could also be held virtually without bothering about the confidentiality of the proceedings which can be ensured by adoption of appropriate security and firewalls.

According to a study, Indian election spending is $8 per vote which is triple of what 60% of Indians survive on any given day. We need to optimise both the cost of a vote and the cost of lives.

10.3 From e-Voting to i-Voting – feasible?

The Election Commission of India announced the dates for the bye-elections in September 2021 after facing a lot of flak from several quarters including the judiciary for having failed to enforce covid-appropriate behaviour in the election process during the last round of Assembly elections. Multiple sets of data have shown that the elections held in the states registered rapid transmission of the virus and subsequent spikes in COVID 19 cases as compared to non-election states. The high positivity rates in some other non-election states were due to other similar mass congregations and other factors. This experience and the possibility that the country could still be fighting some variant of the Covid-19 in 2024 which is able to bypass the current crop of vaccines, makes it imperative that India needs to explore some form of digital democracy in which Internet voting (i-voting) is the first step. If we are moving towards a digital economy why not digital democracy and digital parliament?

Thomas Jefferson once said, 'We do not have government by the majority. We have government by the majority who participate.' So, voter participation is essential to establish the legitimacy and success of any election. In the four assembly states that went to the polls in April 2021, voter turnout decreased in 90% of the 530 seats as compared to the previous Assembly elections in 2016 in these states. Except for Assam, the three—Puducherry, Kerala and Tamil Nadu registered the lowest voter turnout since 2006! A staggering 100% of seats in Puducherry, 95% of seats in Kerala, 90% of seats in Assam and 86% of seats in Tamil Nadu recorded lower turnouts than 2016.The astounding data shows that the pandemic had a significant impact on voter turnout.

i–Voting: Worldwide Experience

i-voting is a system that permits voters to cast their vote from internet-connected computer or device anywhere in the world, including from their homes. A subset of electronic voting (e-voting), it is more cost-effective and feasible as it does not require a specialised devices like an Electronic Voting Machines (EVMs) and designated precincts for voting. Many countries like Estonia, Canada, Australia, Switzerland etc. have undertaken trials allowing i-voting in elections. Amongst these countries, Estonia is the trailblazer with 44% of Estonians using i-voting for casting ballots in an election that allowed hybrid form of voting thereby saving a cumulative of 11,000 working days in each election and 0.75 euros per vote!

History of e-voting in India

India's tryst with electronic voting system started in the 1980s when EVMs were first piloted to replace paper ballot system. The purpose was to cut expenses and strengthen the electoral processes. However, critics argued that, unlike paper ballots, EVMs left no audit trail which meant there was no way to check back if the true intentions of voter were captured, both in situations when the machine malfunctioned or in case, there was a demand from a losing candidate to tally the figures indicated in the EVM with the actual number of voters. It was also argued that people belonging to poor socio-economic backgrounds would face problems in accessing and using the EVMs resulting in large scale disenfranchisement.

Contrary to these assertions, EVMs made voting simple, safe and accessible. In a study conducted in 2016 which analyzed state assembly elections between 1976-2007 it was concluded that EVMs increased voter turnout from marginalized sections such as women, illiterate voters, senior citizens and people belonging to SC/ST community by 6.4%.

Though EVM succeeded in increasing voter turnout, the original concerns regarding tamper-ability, transparency and technical robustness of the machines continue to be highlighted by different political parties despite introduction of Voter Verifiable Paper Audit Trail (VVPAT) and several independent exercises carried out by the Election Commission of India (ECI) proving its efficacy and accuracy.

i-voting in India

To resolve these concerns even more, ECI must work towards introducing i-voting in a phased manner, similar to how EVMs were introduced in the country. Like EVMs, security experts may worry about i-voting's susceptibility to malignant cyber-attacks to substitute or block legitimate votes. However, application of top-end technologies such as distributed ledger technology, commonly known as blockchain, can successfully minimize these risks to a very miniscule level. Estonia has been using blockchain to increase transparency, protect data integrity and secure the sanctity of the votes. In fact, it can be supplemented with a parallel verifiable paper-based trail which can be counted additionally in case the vote difference is less than a prescribed percentage, say 5%.

Research by the Institute for Privy Council Office, Canada suggests that i-voting increases voter turnout in the range of 7-10% especially from people who are hardest to reach such as young voters and the disabled. An added benefit of the system is that it can provide for end-to-end verifiability via cryptographic techniques which means anyone can confirm the accuracy of ballot without relying on election officials.

Conclusion

With the current level of digital divide in the country, it is advisable that a hybrid model of voting allowing i-voting (in cities & towns and urban centre) and EVM voting (elsewhere) could be the starting point for this transformational change. In fact, nascent experimentations to execute i-voting was already attempted by the Telangana State Election Commission in November 2020 in the Greater Hyderabad Municipal Corporation elections for senior citizens and COVID patients enabling them to vote from home. However, the plan was dropped due to legal obstacles.

This innovation will also determine the future vibrancy of democracies all over the world against the very plausible, but uncertain several waves of the current pandemic and may be many such national medical emergencies in future. There is, of course, the additional advantage of saving approximately Rs. 2000 crore towards purchase of new EVMs in our national elections.

CHAPTER 11

TURMOIL IN AFGHANISTAN

11.1 To the Taliban

In August 2021, after the world was stunned by the swift recapture of power by the Talibans in Afghanistan once the United States (US) troops started disengaging themselves, the world continues to watch with bated breath which of their old practices will be reinforced in the country and whether along with the associated misery. The future of the country once again hangs in balance while the average Afghan are haunted by the ghosts of their past. The Taliban had banned girls from education, females were forbidden to work, criminals were publicly executed, and women were stoned to death on alleged charges of adultery, to name a few. The pretext for all these was the implementation of their interpretation of the Shariah Law (Islam's legal system). Soon after returning to power, the Taliban is back to its regressive ways of tightening

* This essay was written soon after the Taliban took over Afghanistan in August 2021

their dominance over women's freedom. Municipality posts held over by women were now being replaced by men representatives; females were being restricted from secondary school education; the new governance in Taliban had no representation from the female community. There had been a lot of protests, predominantly by women ever since Taliban had resurrected to power. While the Taliban administration promised to reassure security and freedom to women, females were still being directed to stay home for their own safety till proper segregation was implemented. There is however no doubt that this is an opportune moment for the Taliban to change history and usher in a new era in the Muslim world which would be etched in history forever.

An opportunity for Taliban to set the record straight

The interpretation of Taliban's Shariah law is different from those of other Islamic countries like the Saudi Arabia, United Arab Emirates, Qatar, Turkey etc. These countries also thrive on the core tenets of Islam while recognising the basic human rights of its people, both men and women. Women in these Islamic countries enjoy legal equality with their male counterparts, access to education and professional opportunities. They are also given the agency to make their own decisions regarding marriage, starting a family, etc. It must be borne in mind that Islamic law from its very inception has given women the legal capacity to make their own decisions post puberty. It recognised the right of women to own and manage property, sue and be sued, to undertake businesses, etc. Interestingly, in the Prophet's (S.A.W) last message to his people, he emphasised on his men the need to be nice and righteous to women. Another anecdote from the Prophet's (S.A.W) life that demonstrated the status attributed to women in Islam was his first marriage to a woman named Khadija (R.A), who was close to 15 years older to him, a business-woman by profession and who proposed marriage to the Prophet (S.A.W) herself. The Taliban's treatment of women in its earlier rule has been the exact opposite of this.

It is about time that the new Taliban, now with its members much younger and having seen how the world and average Afghans cherished every moment of the past 20 years of freedom, change the narrative this time around. Women need to be treated at par with men; they must be encouraged to study and pursue their careers; they must be provided with the agency to marry the person of their choice, and most importantly to not be subject to any discrimination/bias and inhumane/barbaric abuse based on their gender. They should ponder over why Afghans are fleeing their own motherland/country in such high numbers, whether they will be able to provide food, water and shelter to all that they wish to govern and whether they will bring growth and prosperity to their homeland by international trade and commerce or would remain confined to being a pariah state. Even Islam casts a duty on the ruler to provide the basic necessities of life to those they govern.

Hope of a better tomorrow

Spokesperson of the Taliban, Zabihullah Mujahid in the Taliban's first news conference post the takeover vowed to respect and uphold women's rights, encourage women to return to work, girls to schools, private media to remain independent and promised to ensure that terrorism would not thrive in the country. While the claims seemed empowering, the subsequent weeks have seen reports of extra-judicial executions of erstwhile Government officials who worked with the international community, blasts at Jalalabad and Kabul leaving several dead and women-led protests crushed. Promises to restore security in the violence racked country have gone in vain. The general sentiment of the Afghani people currently is not with the Taliban. They fear that the Talibans have not changed in their ways and that explains why thousands of them have been flooding the Kabul Airport over the past month and so to flee the country.

The Taliban administration needs to back its words with actions so as to win over the trust of its people in their administration. They must protect all democratic institutions built by the world in the last 20 years through generous amounts of aid. They shouldn't let capacities for growth and developments wither away. They must rule the country by prioritizing the general sentiment of its people over their own whims and fancies. The best way to win the confidence of people is to usher in some form of democracy via a process of free and fair elections.

Conclusion

The Taliban have currently installed an interim government which is sans any kind of inclusivity as promised during the early days of their capture of Kabul. There are no representatives of women; most of the cabinet are from the Pashtun tribe even though there are several more influential tribes in Afghanistan. The inclusion of globally censured terrorists has further weaned confidence of the international community. However, these are early times. There is still time to rethink and re-focus for the Taliban. The world continues to look at it as a reflection of what Islam stands for. This provides Taliban with the opportunity of a lifetime: it can either show the world the true values of Islam like brotherhood, love, righteousness, equality, and respect for women or it can fall back in a tragic inter-twined set of crises that will take the nation two decades back in its development.

11.2 The US Caused Afghanistan's Development Conundrum

The 31 August, 2021 deadline set by the United States for its complete withdrawal from Afghanistan marks the beginning of an unprecedented era in Asian politics characterized by its unpredictability and shifting geopolitical narratives. It is now widely agreed that America's withdrawal from Afghanistan was ill-timed and appallingly executed. However, a view of its progress (or lack thereof) in Afghanistan indicates that the outcome of this war and the Taliban's ascent into power was a foregone conclusion.

As argued by then President Barack Obama, the infamous troop surge of 2009 was aimed at training competent Afghan National Security Forces (ANSF) for transferring responsibility, ostensibly the beginning of an end to a failing 8-year war. In the surge's aftermath, this goal was partly achieved; ANSF grew in strength, short-term employment was generated, and the Taliban were kept at bay in southern Afghanistan. However, the recent rapid collapse of the ANSF despite over $80 billion invested in their support suggests a larger, more structural issue with US policy in Afghanistan.

Wasted Military Expenditure and 'Capacity-building' in Afghanistan

As is evident through its previous wars (Korea, Vietnam, Iraq among others), US foreign policy has long been guided by the notion that military intervention is a viable solution to most political challenges. Many have criticized this policy as stemming from a sense of hubris, non-recognition of cultural relativism, and refusal to adapt to the changing nature of war. Most modern wars are civil, rooted in ethnic and cultural tensions, consist of more than one 'enemy', and unfold on the battleground of ideas rather than an actual war field. Consequently, fighting these wars should not be through solely military tactics, history necessitates a more nuanced and tailored approach.

This fundamental flaw is preternaturally visible through US' spending in Afghanistan. Renowned economist Jeffrey Sachs notes that out of almost $1 trillion in expenditure by the US, 86% went towards military outlays for US troops, $83 billion on the ANSF, $10 billion on curbing drug trade, and $15 billion on supporting US agencies in Afghanistan – largely sub-contracted to private contractors. Consequently, less than 2% of total US expenditure over 20 years went towards actual nation-building for offsetting the effects of this devastating war. 'Nation-building' here meant supporting counter insurgency efforts, building effective institutions like the legal system etc. Undoubtedly, there has been progress – drafting a constitution for a new political society, building schools, hospitals, and governmental infrastructure.

Despite these bouts of progress, there was one critical issue, most leadership roles within the government and ANSF remained with foreign representatives, all of whom imposed their version of governance on the Afghans. Following their retreat, the country was left in a governance vacuum where nobody truly knew how to lead in institutions that were not built with Afghanistan in mind. An anecdote captured in a 2012 report by the US Government Accountability Office aptly illustrates this conundrum of development transplantation. The USAID issued $130,000 to Afghan contractors who were commissioned to construct a community shower/bathroom with hardly any oversight/accountability. Once deemed ready, authorities found upon inspection that the facility was built 'without holes in the walls/floors for plumbing and drains.' This sounds like a ridiculous, one-off incident until one considers contextual UNICEF statistics; 70% of Afghan people had no access to toilets. As Joel Brinkley asks, if the Afghan contractors had never accessed western-style bathrooms, and were assigned a contract without any oversight, how could they be expected to install something they had no knowledge about?

Misplaced Priorities

Perhaps if the US prioritized capacity-building in Afghanistan from the outset (not as an afterthought to failed military intervention) and focused on working with Afghans instead of treating the government as its proxy and the country as its colony, then there might have been a different outcome. The USA would have mitigated its damage early by seeding a competent government not entirely drunk on foreign aid, and fully comprehensible of the various issues plaguing the country.

Moreover, the US was unable to plug the sources of funding of the various terrorist groups threatening the democratic

Afghan government. Not only was a unitary central government at odds with the ground realities in Afghanistan, but the US's misplaced priorities (focusing on Taliban strongholds instead of preventing the influx of Pakistani militants; not securing major cities like Kabul; reduced focus on regions with less Taliban influence) also accelerated the democratic decline.

Attempts now seem focused on damage control and shifting narratives, rather than accepting resounding failure. The narrative now propounded that the ANSF chose not to fight for their country is reductive and appears to be an exercise in obfuscation. The US was well aware that the ANSF had an overall literacy rate of 14% and extremely high attrition. In the absence of education, expecting illiterate members of the security forces to engage with sophisticated US military equipment or even read through equipment manuals and calculate missile trajectories is out of the question. The issue was structural and the US policy over the past 20 years clearly failed in this regard. Post-conflict reconstruction must account for such nuances.

Looking Forward

There is a now-proven saying in Afghanistan: *the Americans have the watches, but Taliban has the time.* While there is no scope for turning back the clock, it is paramount for the international community to create an environment for re-building an Afghanistan that is not a petri dish for deadlier threats; that values fundamental human rights, and recognizes that it does not need Western-style governance to prosper.

[illegible]

Recommend[illegible]

[illegible]

The Bank [illegible]

[illegible]

PRAISE FOR THE BOOK

Resource mobilisation and decentralised approach towards handing the crisis while keeping focus on inclusive growth alive, has been a herculean task. Amar Patnaik highlights Odisha's lessons in Covid governance which he calls the Odisha Model. In the wake of the pandemic, the government did advance disbursement of welfare resources to entitled beneficiaries, and the Panchayats emerged as central to the state's communication and implementation strategy. This book will hugely contribute to cooperative federalism.

Dr Vijay L Kelkar

Chairman, 13th Finance Commission

The book presents a realistic assessment of the impact of the pandemic, the role played by the Odisha Government in handling the concerns that emerged about data privacy and protection and the role of played by Panchayats as central to implementing the policy decisions taken by the state. Evolving and dynamic governance structure in the state helped mitigate the impact of the pandemic.

Sameer Kochhar

Chairman, SKOCH Group

Social life came under deep stress due to pandemic. Life would have come to a grinding halt but for technology and digitalisation. The book is an excellent commentary on the new paradigm that has the potential to impact future. The book highlights the debate between Right to Life vs Right to Privacy and emphasises that any data protection body must be abundantly independent. Author's stress on one data policy is a valid argument and I feel it is essential towards protecting privacy in India.

Dr Gulshan Rai

Former National Cyber Security Coordinator

A timely book from someone who is not just an essential part of the legislative but has also years of first-hand experience of governance in an executive role and has a deep understanding of the country. The book throws light on India's covid management - right from testing, tracing and treating to ensuring a billion plus Indians got their vaccines. The author has through his essays, given an overview of his state's work during COVID. Right from migration issues to female labour force participation and emancipation, and education are well captured. This is a book which must be read for the excellent insights it provides from the space of policy for disaster preparedness. A handy guide for law makers to gauge, understand and tackle the new-age challenges to India's economy whether in health, tech, education, agriculture.

Priyanka Chaturvedi

MP, Rajya Sabha

Pandemic Disruptions and Odisha's Lessons in Governance is undoubtedly a topical and neoteric source as it deals with the impact of the COVID-19 crisis and the resultant mitigation responses. Divided into eleven chapters, this seminal piece covers a broad range of themes such as health, technology, data protection, women and child rights, environment, economy, democracy and transgender rights, the state of Odisha and its governance. The book presents an authentic overview of COVID-19 crisis management and responses. It presents to the reader insightful commentaries on current issues of prominence such as the right to privacy, the inclusive growth model, artificial intelligence, blockchain technology, elections in the pandemic, corruption and unrest in Afghanistan. Due to its comprehensive coverage of topics and lucid writing style, this book is a significant contribution to understanding the concerns that India is facing. It is an essential resource for anyone who is interested in public policy- planning and implementation.

Professor Rekha Saxena
Department of Political Science, University of Delhi